CONTENTS

Part One

Part Two

FIFTY EXPERIENTIAL EXERCISES

Part Three

EXPERIENTIAL EDUCATION

Laboratory Learning

A new model of learning has developed in America over the past twenty-five years, often called sensitivity training, and now better known as laboratory learning. Laboratory learning is a group experience that provides participants with opportunities to learn more about themselves, their feelings and behaviors. It involves interpersonal experiences which can be analyzed in terms of generalizations and applications for "back-home" living.

The optimum atmosphere in laboratory learning is one of mutual trust and authenticity in which learners can behave with a minimum of defensiveness. Laboratory learning combines experiential learning and conceptualization, including the examination of one's values, attitudes and behaviors, and their effects upon self and others.

A commonly accepted assumption about effective learning in a laboratory setting is that the most long-lasting learnings are those which affect a person as a whole, including mind, emotions, body awareness and spirituality. As William Schutz pointed out, "man is a unified being and functions on many levels at once: physical, emotional, intellectual, inter-personal, social and spiritual. These levels are intimately interrelated, and actions on any one level are inevitably accompanied by actions on all others."[1]

Terms such as "affective education" or "confluent education" are becoming popular. They stress the emotional, or feeling component, of the educational process, as well as the cognitive. In a setting of laboratory education, where personal growth is the goal, feelings are recognized and dealt with openly. Only through greater awareness of one's feelings can the learner choose to express, or postpone expression of, the feelings which well up within. To deny or repress them prevents learning. An open and safe climate in which the learner can risk admitting and expressing deep emotions is the most cogenial atmosphere in which human growth takes place.

Another assumption in laboratory education is that learning implies changing attitudes, values and behaviors, and not merely rote memorization of facts and information. Accepting a new viewpoint about life, about self, about the world or a new way of acting and relating, are the most significant ways in which a person can change. Alfred H. Gorman defines learning simply as "a change in behavior."[2]

The final assumption about laboratory learning is the most crucial of all, that the best learning is based on experience. Modern methodologies of experience-based learning are derived largely from the pioneering work

of John Dewey whose viewpoint was that people learn after reflecting upon
and evaluating their life experience.[3] The school and the classroom are
artificial devices for helping children learn. Insofar as the classroom is
a microcosm of the outside world it can succeed in constituting a wholesome
environment in which significant learning may take place. But most class-
rooms are places for lecturing and reading and testing rather than experiencing.

Laboratory education succeeds insofar as it simulates life outside. The
difference will be in the safety and openness of the laboratory atmosphere.
The facilitator may introduce a structured experience, which is then followed
by discussing and evaluating the experience to see what learnings might derive
from it and how these learnings can be applied to life.

John E. Jones and J. William Pfeiffer, directors of University Associates,
a consulting and publishing firm which trains human relations trainers, have
published a series of twelve volumes on the theory and practice of experience-
based learning, including handbooks and collections of structured experiences.[4]
They conceptualize a continuum of learning from the least experiential to the
most experiential in ten stages. These are, in order of increasingly
experiential learning:

> reading
> lecture
> experiential lecture
> discussion
> participation training
> case study
> role playing
> instrumentation
> structured experience
> intensive growth group

It is the contention of the University Associates leadership that in the more
experiential approaches, stressing active participant involvement instead of
passive receptivity, "the learning is presumably internalized more effectively."[5]

Structured Experiences

It often appears that anyone may conduct an experiential education program, since no formal lecture is involved and learning emerges from the participation of the group. This is definitely not so, however. Unless adequately trained facilitators utilize these structured experiences, in all probability only a small part of their potential effects will be realized. In such a case these experiences become more sophisticated parlor games than meaningful educational activities. The structured experiences are basically means to an end, not ends in themselves, i. e., not just "fun and games."

Effective facilitators of experiential education should be persons who radiate confidence, have a disciplined approach to goal-setting and directionality in realizing the goals, sensitivity and warmth to create a supportive atmosphere, and an enthusiastic approach to laboratory education. They should be persons with adequate administrative skills to enable the group to move forward in a well-ordered fashion and create confidence in them as trustworthy authorities, and should be effective discussion leaders since much of the ultimate learning flows out of the reflective dialog and group discussion following the structured experiences.

The following five steps should be utilized in carrying out an experiential learning model:[6]

1) Experiencing

   The structured experience is carried out with the guidance of the facilitator

2) Publishing

   Participants "publish" their reactions and observations with others who have participated together with them or observed them

3) Processing

   After sharing reactions and observations, the dynamics that emerged from the experience are explored, discussed and evaluated (processed)

4) Generalizing

   This involves extracting general principles from the experience, a statement of learnings which help define and clarify the experience

5) Applying

   Once general principles are derived, it is crucial that some attempt be made to apply them to the lives of the participants.

FOOTNOTES

1. <u>Here Comes Everybody</u> (N.Y.: Harper & Row, Harrow Books, 1972), p. xviii.

2. <u>Teachers and Learners: The Interactive Process of Education</u> (Boston: Allyn & Bacon, 1974), p. 13.

3. <u>Experience and Education</u> (N.Y.: Macmillan, 1959), esp. chapter 8, "Experience: The Means and Goal of Education."

4. <u>Annual Handbooks for Group Facilitators</u> (La Jolla, Ca.: University Associates, 1972, 1973, 1974, 1975, 1976, 1977); and <u>Handbook of Structured Experiences for Human Relations Training</u>, Volumes I-VI (La Jolla, CA: University Associates, 1973-1977).

5. John E. Jones and J. William Pfeiffer, <u>Reference Guide to Handbooks and Annuals</u> (La Jolla, Ca.: University Associates, 1975), p. 1.

6. <u>Ibid.</u>, pp. 1-5.

JUDAISM AND THE HUMAN POTENTIAL MOVEMENT

An Outline of Theoretical Assumptions

I)   Hasidism

Joy, song, dance, prayer
Freedom, spontaneity, letting go
Feelings
Creativity
Kavana, mysticism, spirituality, here-and-now, meditation
Sanctity (Kedushah) - sparks
Authenticity, realness
Absence of dichotomies
       ritual-ethics
       sacred-profane
       knowledge-fervor
       halacha-agada

II)   Reconstructionism

Democracy (women's rights)
Reason, Science, Empiricism
Freedom
       vote, not a veto
       no "shoulds"
       mitzvot - yes; averot - no
Experimentation
Growth, evolution
       Judaism: evolving, religious civilization
Holistic; civilization (not just religion, culture, folk)
Community, peoplehood, covenant
History-sancta-experience

III)   Humanistic Psychology and Education

Experience
Responsibility
Values
Affective & Cognitive
Community
Here & Now
Resacralization
Holism; mind-body
Growth - human potential;
       Self-actualization;
       goodness of persons;
       capacity to change & grow

Resources on Experiential Learning

Educational Change - A Humanistic Approach
  Ed. Ray Eiben and Al Milliren
  University Associates, 1976

Clarifying Jewish Values - Values Activities for Jewish Groups
  Dov Peretz Elkins
  Growth Associates, 1977

Teaching People To Love Themselves - A Leader's Handbook of
  Theory and Technique for Self-Esteem and Affirmation Training
  Dov Peretz Elkins
  Growth Associates, 1977

Experiential Education: X-ED
  John & Lela Hendrix
  Abingdon, 1975

Joining Together - Group Theory and Group Skills
  David W. Johnson and Frank P. Johnson
  Prentice-Hall, 1975

A Handbook of Structured Experiences for Human Relations Training
  Ed. J. William Pfeiffer and John E. Jones
  University Associates, Volumes I-VI, 1972-77

The Annual Handbook for Group Facilitators
  Ed. J. William Pfeiffer and John E. Jones
  University Associates, 1972-77 (Six volumes to date)

A Humanistic Psychology of Education - Making the School Everybody's House
  Richard A. Schmuck and Patricia A. Schmuck
  National Press Books, 1974

Affective Education - Strategies for Experiential Learning
  Ed. Louis Thayer
  University Associates

*****

Important addresses for books and workshops on experiential education:

University Associates
7596 Eads Avenue
La Jolla, CA. 92037

National Humanistic Education Center
110 Spring St.
Saratoga Springs, NY 12866

Institute for Humanistic and
    Transpersonal Education
New England Center
Box 575
Amherst, MA. 01002

Alternatives in Religious Education
1110 Holly Oak Circle
San Jose, CA. 95120

*****

Name Tag

This is a get acquainted activity. Each person is given a 5 x 8 card. In the center section of the card the person writes his first name in large letters with magic marker. The leader instructs the participants to write their name large enough to be seen across the room. It is best if the leader makes his own name tag on a flip chart or chalkboard so that the participants see how it is done. At the left top of the name tag, the participants write the name of a Jewish hero whom they admire. At the left bottom of the name tag participants write a significant date in their Jewish life such as Bar Mitzvah, Hebrew High school graduation, wedding, etc. At the right top of the name tag participants write whether they are Orthodox, Conservative or Reform. If any of the members belong to the same synagogue, instead of that participants can write the name of a city or other place in Israel where they would like to live. In the right bottom corner of the name tag, participants write two or three words which signify to them important Jewish values such as: Kashrut, Shabbat, social justice, learning, etc.

Each person then puts his name tag on his chest either with masking tape or safety pin and is asked to walk around the room looking at as many name tags as possible. One effective way to do this is to ask people to do "silent milling". By walking around the room silently and looking at other people's name tags they will not be inclined to stop for very long but move from person to person.

One possible way to continue this getting acquainted exercise is to then ask persons after two or three minutes of milling around the room to freeze and look around the room. They are then asked to find one other person to sit down with and share the contents of their name tags. Still another possibility is to find one other person to share just one of the corners of the name tag during a two minute period, each person having one or two minutes to talk. Then each person finds a new partner and shares another corner of the name tag, and then again after two minutes of sharing, persons can find a third partner and then a fourth partner each time sharing a different corner of the name tag. At that point each person will have gotten to know at least four others on an individual basis.

The name tag can be used in a variety of other ways, such as have members of the group add to the name tag at various points in the life of the group. For example; in the top center of the name tag each person can write the names of two or three people whom they met and whose friendship they would like to develop subsequent to that meeting. In the center bottom of the name tag each person can write one experience in the group that he enjoyed or learned a great deal from. Other possibilities may also come to mind as the group develops. In large groups it is important to remind participants to constantly bring their name tags to group sessions so that everyone will be able to address each other with first names. This is very important in creating a strong group spirit, and makes persons feel at home, accepted and comfortable. These are crucial goals for the establishment of the proper atmosphere for effective experiential learning.

The Name Game

This is another getting acquainted activity which may seem formidable but in reality is not that difficult and can be a great deal of fun. Persons sit in a circle of not more than fifteen. If there are more than fifteen in the room, then small groups of ten to fifteen can be formed. The first person anywhere in the group begins by saying his name and the name of a Jewish hero that he admires. This can be the name that he wrote on his tag in the preceeding activity. For example I would say my name is Dov and I admire Abba Eban. The next person to the right starts by saying the name of the hero of the previous person and then says his own name and hero. For example the second person would say to the person on his left, "This is Dov and he admires Abba Eban, my name is Bob and I admire Golda Meir." The third person again begins at the beginning repeating both of the previous persons' names and heros and then adds his own. Each succeeding person continues in the same fashion starting from the beginning saying the name of each person and his hero going around the circle and then adding his own.

There may well be some fear and anxiety when the leader explains this exercise because people feel that they are being put on the spot to remember so many names and heros. However, experience shows that most people can easily remember this number of names even though initially they believe they might not be able to. The leader may also assure participants that if they forget a name or a hero, other members of the group can assist them. This is not a contest or a memory examination, just an enjoyable getting acquainted exercise without pressure or too much seriousness attached to it. The leader can model the lightness of the exercise by treating it in a way that helps people relax and enjoy themselves.

By the end of this exercise participants will know the names of the members of their small group of ten to fifteen as well as some value of the persons from the Jewish heros they admire.

Other possibilities, instead of mentioning the name of the hero, are mentioning a favorite Jewish ritual, a favorite Jewish holiday, a favorite Hebrew prayer, a favorite Jewish book, a book read recently, one's Hebrew name, or a variety of other possibilities. There is, obviously, no one right way to perform this getting acquainted exercise.

If the group is large, this exercise might be repeated at the beginning of each day. If it is an on-going group, use different   groupings so that participants come to know others beside the initial ten or fifteen with whom they did this activity the first time.

(Of course if the name tag exercise had been used prior to this name game, name tags should be removed before beginning this activity).

Hebrew Names

This exercise can be used as a getting acquainted activity or at some other point in the life of the group when it seems appropriate to share more of one's background, heritage and personal life experiences.

Small groups of five to ten persons should be formed and each person is asked to tell his Hebrew name. In some cases this might be a Yiddish name. Often people do not distinguish between Hebrew and Yiddish names and it is not important for the purpose of this exercise to make any such distinction. Along with telling the Hebrew name the individual is asked to tell something about that name. For example: For whom is the person named, such as a grandparent, uncle, aunt or other relative. What does that person mean to this individual? What does the person know about the individual after whom they are named, if anything? What significance does that person, that grandparent or other relative, have in the life of this person's family? Where did he or she live? Where was he or she born? What other details are known about the person that might have some relevance to the individual who now holds that Hebrew name?

Another area which the person speaking might discuss is whether that name is the original name given by his parents or one that he adopted at a later point in life. Often in religious school a teacher will assign a person a Hebrew name if that individual is not familiar with the one that he received at birth. How did the person get that name? On what basis did the teacher choose that Hebrew name. Does it sound like his English name? Is it perhaps a translation of his English name, or does it have some other significance?

Still a third possible area of discussion can be what associations does the person have with any person in the Bible, or prominent in Jewish history, who may have had that name? What qualities, traits and characteristics about that famous individual does this person admire or want to emulate? What life experiences or well-known facts about such a bibical or historical personality are significant to this modern day namesake?

Another area upon which the individual may elaborate is: Are there any associations in the person's life that come to mind when thinking of one's Hebrew name? For example: being called to the Torah by that name or playing a role in a play by that name or some other life experience that revolves around the person's Hebrew name.

Still another possibility is this: Would that person choose that name were he able to choose his own Hebrew name today? Does he like the name or does he not like the name? What about it does he like or dislike? What Hebrew name would he choose if he were free to choose his own?

All of the above questions help individuals to share parts of themselves by discussing their Hebrew name and its significance to them. They are in essence talking about their life, their values, their experiences, their family

background and many things that reveal part of their total personality.
Such disclosure helps people to get to know one another and fosters an
attitude of warmth and acceptance in the group. In addition it helps
participants feel comfortable and at home since they know others and
others know them. Furthermore the tone of the group has been established
by sharing some of their Hebrew roots and other aspects of their Jewish
heritage. Far ranging discussions have spun off from this type of activity
getting into areas of Jewish history, literature, family values and other
important realms of discussion and personal sharing.

Self-Disclosure

This is a getting-acquainted exercise. It helps group members feel closer to one another, and to feel more deeply the true sense of Klal Yisrael, of covenant community.

People generally have a longing to be close to others. There is a natural tendency to crave intimacy within all of us. Yet, experience, being hurt, and societal norms, often prevent us from opening ourselves to our neighbors and friends. We erect walls of armor around ourselves and prevent others from knowing who we really are (See Father Powell's powerful little book, WHY AM I AFRAID TO TELL YOU WHO I REALLY AM?).

The leader explains that this exercise will help people get to know one another better, and help form a closer group. He reads the following quotation from Elie Wiesel's book, Souls on Fire (Random House, 1972, p. 33):

"Every encounter quickens the steps of the Redeemer: let two beings become one and the world is no longer the same: let two human creatures accept one another and creation will have meaning, the meaning they will have imposed upon it. That is the new idea introduced into Jewish life by Hasidism."

He then explains that he will hand out a sheet with a list of adjectives. Each person is to circle five of the words that best describe himself.

After a few minutes, participants form groups of four and each person takes a turn explaining a self-description.

A next possible step would be to have members of each small group add other deserved positive adjectives to other persons in their group. This might not be possible in a new group, but can be used effectively if group members know each other somewhat.

Finally, the leader calls on several members of the group at large to receive general reactions about what this experience was like. A discussion can then be held about how people get to know one another, about the benefits and dangers of becoming vulnerable, and about the process of intimacy and group solidarity.

Self-Disclosure Sheet

unforgiving   thoughtless

      out-going   suspicious   constant

easily-approachable   care-free   solitary

    opinionated   shy   easily hurt

fickle   interested   good-natured   easy-going   selfish

   concerned   serious   easily led   cold

affectionate   loyal   slow to relate   aggressive

dependent   obliging   trusting   independent

argumentative   selective   generous   fun-loving

interesting   dependable   likeable   reserved

  compromising   selfish   truthful   unpredictable

humorous   shallow   light hearted   dynamic

   stand-offish   indifferent

Visualization

This exercise is also one that promotes a group closeness and strong feelings of Jewish identity. Participants are asked to sit back, relax, and close their eyes. They are then asked to try to relax their body, to let go of any tension in their muscles and to feel very comfortable and serene. The leader then instructs the participants to visualize a white light surrounding their heart. Each time they breathe in the light gets stronger, and as they breathe out the light remains the same strength and does not wane. The leader then asks the participants to continue visualizing the white light as it begins to spread all around the body and into the head. At that point the white light emerges from the top of the head and forms a beam which goes to the center of the ceiling in the room. Each person then visualizes a white beam of light emerging from all of the heads of the other people in the room joined together at the center of the ceiling. Then all of the lights merging together at the top of the ceiling go further upwards out of the building and join together with the white lights coming from other Jews in the same city or community. This white light then binds all of the people together in one common fellowship. The leader asks participants to continue visualizing the white light so that now it joins together with the beams of other white lights of other Jewish communities in the state (such as Pennsylvania, New York, California, etc.).

Now the white lights join together with those of Jewish communities throughout the United States, so that we all feel a close sense of unity with Jews throughout America. Now the pool of white light emerging from Jewish communities throughout North America join with all the pools of white lights shining from other Jewish communities throughout the world in Russia, Israel, Europe, Africa and elsewhere. So that now all of the Jewish people living in the entire world come together by these strong white lights unifying us into one universal family.

Now visualize Jews from past generations and past centuries still emitting a strong white light, joining with those of this generation so that a sense of unity with world Jewry of the past is also felt by the members of the group.

At this point the leader asks the group to continue visualizing this white light joining the Jews throughout the world, past and present, and to see what feelings, thoughts and experiences emerge for that person.

The leader then says to the group, "Now, realizing that we may return to visualize this unifying beam of universal white light at any time we wish, let it now fade from our minds and whenever we are ready, open our eyes and return to this room." At this point the leader lets persons sit with their feelings for a moment or so of quietness. When the group seems ready, the leader asks some individuals to share their thoughts and feelings about this experience of being unified with Jews throughout the world. For some it may have been a very positive, inspiring experience, for others it might have been without significant meaning. There is no one right way to have had this experience and the leader should be careful not to judge those who at that moment may not have successfully visualized in the way he wanted them to.

A group discussion may now take place regarding the feeling of unity with Jewish people past and present.

A Pen Pal

The leader explains or reminds the group of the old custom of having a pen pal in a foreign country. (Someone with whom one corresponds through the mail though the parties have never met in person.) This is often practiced in schools or other institutions to help persons find out about life in different cultures.

The leader then tells the group, "Imagine that each of you has been corresponding with a pen pal over the past few months. In the recent letter from your pen pal he writes: I see that you mention that you are Jewish. In my country there is no such thing as a Jew. Can you please explain to me, what is a Jew?"

The leader then gives out paper and pencil or pen and tells the members of the group, "We now have approximately ten minutes to compose a reply to our pen pal. Write him a letter explaining to him what is a Jew. You might want to include some of the holidays, customs, ceremonies, rituals. In addition some of the values, and behaviors and experiences that relate to Jewishness in your view. You may also want to relate some of your family experiences of being Jewish and what being Jewish means to you personally. It is good to combine factual material such as history, holidays, laws, etc. with some of your own personal likes and dislikes, preferences and values regarding the Jewish heritage."

Participants then proceed to write a letter to their pen pal. After the ten minutes the leader asks the group to take another minute to wind up and conclude whatever they are writing.

At this point several options are available. The leader may ask four or five persons to read their letter and then a group discussion may follow making points of comparison and contrast between the various letters read.

Another possibility is to break the group into smaller groups of four or six and instead of reading the entire letter, ask group members to pick out two things from their letter that they think their pen pal would be most interested in hearing about and share just those things with the members of the small group. At that point the leader may ask for several volunteers to summarize some of the most interesting things people assume their pen pals would have been interested in.

At that point the leader may ask for two or three people to share their whole letter if anyone feels so inclined.

A general discussion may then follow about any left over points or questions.

A good way to conclude this exercise is by having individuals write three or four sentences beginning with the words, "I learned....", I discovered....", or "I became aware that...." In this way participants distill from the experience some of the major learning that emerged from experience of summarizing Judaism to their pen pal. The "I learned...." statements can be used effectively at the conclusion of many of the exercises in the Jewish Consciousness Raising programs.

Scanning Pleasant Memories

This activity has many positive benefits. One of the most effective uses it has is to help members of a group to become familiar with one another by sharing personal memories. It is an excellent exercise to use at the beginning of a group meeting when people have many other things on their mind and are coming from many different places and they are not yet ready to give their full attention to the matters at hand.

Participants are asked to form small groups of four or five with each person taking one minute to share a pleasant memory about a specific subject which the leader designates. The subject matter will often depend on the season of the year such as a coming holiday or special event. For example: the leader may say, if the festival of Pesach is coming soon, "Each person take one minute to share a pleasant memory regarding a Seder that he recalls from childhood."

Another possible topic is a visit to Israel, or some experience in childhood regarding the State of Israel. Other possible topics are a pleasant learning experience either in a class room or lecture hall; some Jewish book that one read and enjoyed; a meaningful spiritual experience in prayer; or some similar events.

Another possibility is to ask participants to think of some of the important Yiddish or Hebrew or English value words that were used in their home regarding Jewishness or Judaism. Or one might ask the group members to think of some highlight milestone, such as a Bris, Bar/Bat Mitzvah, wedding, etc..

By getting in touch with some of these important memories and the feelings associated with them individuals are tapping the huge resource of positive Jewish associations which reinforces their current Jewish identity. It also helps them become clear on present Jewish values, attitudes, commitments and loyalities. Another significance in sharing these memories is that of establishing a positive atmosphere of warmth and acceptance among the members of the group.

The "Scanning Pleasant Memories" activity can help create the right kind of mood for another important part of the program. If the general theme of the meeting deals with some specific issue or holiday or other related Jewish theme, a good way to get into that subject is by drawing upon memories of the past that focus attention on that issue and help participants become interested in pursuing it further in a different fashion. It is important to give a specific time limit for each person in the group to share his memories so that the story telling does not become overly long and boring, permitting individual members to go on and on at the expense of the group. Within stipulated time limits this exercise can be extremely meaningful, pleasant and growth producing.

Four Corners

This is a value clarification exercise which helps participants to make decisions choosing among alternatives and publicly declaring their stand.

The leader places four signs or posters on the walls in four corners of the room indicating four possible ideological positions regarding a major Jewish issue. Participants are asked to walk and stand near the sign which most closely resembles their own opinion. It is not necessary to agree in totality with that position. Rather, the participants should choose the one out of the four choices which is closest to their own thinking.

Some examples of four corner signs would be:

1. Intermarriage

    a. Send him to the Rabbi
    b. Be privately depressed
    c. Show continual displeasure
    d. Tell him "its your decision"

2. Priorities in Jewish education

    a. Hebrew language
    b. Ethics
    c. History
    d. Shabbat and holy days

3. Defining the Jewish people

    a. an international people
    b. a religious group
    c. a nationalist-political entity
    d. a cultural-ethnic group

The leader may design his own four choices on any major issue relating to the group at hand and current major concerns. These should be clear choices and be a controversial topic so that a fair distribution among the four signs is possible. If all of the participants were to go to one or two of the four corners of the room, that would remove the challenge and excitement from the exercise. Thus careful selection in the choices is required.

The leader should give the following instructions to the group (after which the leader reads the four choices). " You will be asked in a moment to select the opinion which most closely resembles your own and to walk to that corner of the room. At that point you will discuss with the other people who made a similar choice the reasons for your selections, each person having a time to share his own opinions. It will be necessary to appoint a spokesperson for each of the four groups so that after ten or fifteen minutes of discussion I will ask each group to have a summary of their opinions presented to the entire group by the spokesperson. Are there any questions?"

After the group has discussed the issue for ten or fifteen minutes with each person having had a turn to speak and the spokesperson organizing a brief summary, the leader then calls upon each person in turn to present the summary to the entire group. (It is often convenient at this point to ask the members of the group to sit down rather than stand during the entire discussion).

After these four positions have been presented, the leader may then open the floor for total group discussion asking anyone to refute, disagree with or challenge any of the summarized opinions of the other three groups.

Another option at this point would be to ask the members of the total group to make a second selection, having now heard arguments and counter agruments on all four positions. At that point the leader would ask those who went to different corners after having heard the discussion to raise their hands to see how many changed, and how many were influenced by the previous discussion.

What Is A Jew?

There are several important purposes for this exercise. One is to draw upon the creative talents and abilities of the members. Formal education rarely capitalizes upon the tremendous store of talent, imagination and creativity of students. When persons participate in a creative activity, they draw upon the full range of their own resources, including intellectual, cultural, emotional, physical and spiritual. The second major purpose for this exercise is to reach more deeply into the lower levels of consciousness of the participants. Among Freud's great contributions to our understanding of human nature is that there are levels of thought, preception and imagination beyond the verbal level. Having persons compose a drawing, write a song, or create some non-verbal expression of their inner feelings and thoughts taps more deeply the profound recesses of the human psyche than other means.

Participants are given a large piece of newsprint or construction paper and magic markers and/or other drawing implements, and are asked to make a drawing of their conception what is a Jew? This should be done as far as possible without words on the drawing or as few words as possible. People are left to conceptualize in an image what Judaism and the Jewish people mean to them.

Another alternative is to ask the person to write a song if he is musically inclined. Still another possibility is to compose a poem. While this is a verbal creation, it nevertheless draws more upon the artistic, so called "right-brain" function, of the personality. This reaches more deeply into the mystical, spiritual, imaginative aspect of that individual.

At the end of the exercise one possible way to process the creations is to form small groups with each person sharing his creation and explaining it to the members of the small group. Alternatively the members of the small group may offer their own interpretations followed by the explanation of the creator.

Another possibility is to have a parade of drawings, songs, poems, etc. around the room with everyone holding his up before the group one at a time with the entire group marching around the room in parade style. The person who reaches the front of the room stops, holds up the painting, or drawing or poem or song, and displays it before the group. The group then moves on and the next person coming to the front, stops and displays his creation.

Drawings, poems, songs may be placed on a bulletin board for permanent display.

The Ideal Synagogue

This exercise is similar to the preceding one in that it requires imagination, fantasy and non-verbal creativity.

Participants are asked to draw the ideal synagogue using as few words as possible, if any. The leader may suggest in a very broad fashion some of the possible areas for drawing, being careful not to influence the specific details of the drawing. For example, what parts of the synagogue will receive major emphasis? The school, the worship sanctuaries, the meeting halls, smaller rooms for small group meetings, conferences, offices? What part will the outdoors play in this synagogue? Where and how will the functionaries perform their duties, such as Rabbi, Cantor, educator, social worker, administrator, etc.? How many floors will the building have? What size, shape and style windows? What colors? What materials? What will be the main functions of the synagogue? How will people approach the building and leave it? How will the sanctuary be organized? Where will the ark, the Bimah, the seats, all be located? Participants should be reminded that there are no limits to the possibilities which their imagination might conjure up. They should not be guided merely by past recollections of buildings and congregations with which they are familiar.

This exercise can be processed in some of the same ways in which the previous one was. Namely, through small group sharing, parade style, total group sharing and/or bulletin board displays.

Enough time should be given to conceive, draw, describe, and discuss the ideal synagogue so that the full impact of the exercise may be felt. It often produces enormously creative ideas and excites the participants about the possibilities of recreating and redesigning a new kind of American synagogue.

Another possibility following all of the above might be to collate a list of some of the more creative and imaginative ideas from each of the various synagogue designs and make one composite group design. Alternatively, a list of some of the more clever innovations might be made and these could be pursued with various community or synagogue leaders.

I Am A Jew

This exercise utilizes a very beautiful poem/statement written by the prominent European Jewish thinker, Edmond Fleg. Fleg's piece, called, "I Am A Jew", has been reprinted in many anthologies and prayer books and is a very effective statement of what it means to be a Jew.

The leader distributes copies of Fleg's statement and asks each participant to rank-order the five most important sentences of the ten which Fleg lists. He then asks the group to delete two of the five leaving three. After giving time to do that the leader then asks the group to form small groups of four. After the quartets (groups of four) are formed they are broken into two groups of two. Each person in this dyad (group of two) discusses his number one choice and explains why he made that selection. After two minutes for each person these dyads are broken up and each person finds a new partner within his quartet, this time discussing priority number two on his list of three. Then, finally, a third partnership is formed out of the same quartet and each person discusses choice number three.

The next step is for the entire quartet to rejoin and each person shares one or two of the choices that were eliminated after the leader requested that numbers four and five be deleted. Finally any unfinished business or left over questions may be discussed in the quartet.

The leader may then turn to the entire group and ask for some "I learned...." statements.

I AM A JEW

I am a Jew because the faith of Israel demands of me no
abdication of the mind.

> I am a Jew because the faith of Israel requires of me
> all the devotion of my heart.

I am a Jew because in every place where suffering weeps, the
Jew weeps.

> I am a Jew because at every time when despair cries out,
> the Jew hopes.

I am a Jew because the word of Israel is the oldest and the
newest.

> I am a Jew because the promise of Israel is the universal
> promise.

I am a Jew because, for Israel, the world is not yet completed:
men are completing it.

> I am a Jew because, for Israel, man is not created: men
> are creating him.

I am a Jew because, above the nations and Israel, Israel places
Man and his Unity.

> I am a Jew because, above Man, image of the divine Unity,
> Israel places the unity which is divine.

Edmond Fleg, Dynamics of
Emancipation

ACTIVITY NUMBER 37

Hooray For Me

One of the most important aspects of Jewish Consciousness Raising is giving a participant a sense of pride and satisfaction in his Jewish heritage. Minority groups have great difficulty accepting themselves and seeing themselves as full and equal members of society. Very often the opinions and attitudes of majority groups are internalized by members of minority groups such as Jews, Blacks, Indians, Puerto Ricans, Chicanos, etc. The reader may refer to the author's collection, Proud To Be Me, to find many statements describing the self-hatred that is so pervasive in modern Jewish society.

Milton Steinberg's chapter, "The Sick Soul", deals most effectively with this subject. The reader may also want to refer to the author's book, Teaching People To Love Themselves, Chapter Seven, "Self-esteem for Minority Groups".

In this exercise the group is asked to stand in a circle and one person comes to the center of the circle. Another possibility is, in larger groups, for one person to come up to the front of the group and stand before them. The person is instructed to say one sentence, "I am a Jew" and then the group will applaud and cheer for forty-five seconds.

The spirit of the exercise is very important and the leader's active participation, modeling great enthusiasm, will go a long way toward insuring its success.

At first blush this seems to be a very artificial and perhaps even childish activity. However, it is not, except in the best sense of the word "childish". The psychological effect of this experience on the participant can be enormous. Being a Jew is often a source of embarrassment for people. This exercise gives the focus person an opportunity to be applauded, cheered and affirmed solely for being a member of the Jewish people. Its effects can be quite dramatic.

At the end of the exercise the focus person is asked to describe how he felt while that was happening, what thoughts were going through his head and what feelings emerged within him.

A second and third person may then volunteer to participate and to see how the experience effects him. That person (persons) may then describe his (their) experience.

Qualities in the Jewish People

The leader gathers a large collection of different kinds of fruit; apples, oranges, bananas, grapes and whatever else is available at that particular season of the year. The fruit is placed on a table in the center of the room and participants are asked to approach the table and select one piece of fruit. After the fruit has been taken, the leader tells the members of the group that they will be asked to examine their piece of fruit and make some comparisons between it and the Jewish people.

For example: One person who selected an apple might look it over and say: "Its red color reminds me of the strength and courage of our people. Its shiny surface reminds me of the brightness and the intellectual superiority of the contributions made by our people." Another person might select a piece of fruit with a blemish and be reminded of some of the problems that we still face. Another individual may relate to the size, shape or color, the contours, ripeness and other qualities.

The effect of this exercise is to bring out feelings and values that persons can more easily share and more easily become aware of through the medium of describing this piece of fruit. Often it will uncover ideas, information and emotions that ordinarily lie beneath the surface. In addition, that person will have an opportunity to publicly affirm his ties, loyalties and commitments to his people, his admiration and respect, as well as his disappointment in, the Jewish people.

The group is broken into small groups of six and each person in the group shows his piece of fruit to the other members and explains the qualities and characteristics that he identifies with the Jewish people.

At the conclusion of that segment of the exercise participants might be asked to discuss which of the qualities they mentioned in the previous whip around they themselves possess, such as courage, creativity, high ethical values, sensitivity, etc. and which they do not possess. A third whip around the circle of six might be to have each person select the one major characteristic of the Jewish people about which he is most proud and explain why he feels that way.

Still another possible whip around would involve having group members select one quality or characteristic of the Jewish people which this person would like to see developed more, perhaps relating some recent incident in which leaders or large segments of our people manifested a lack of a certain quality or another.

Feeling Reactions

This exercise involves getting participants to be more in touch with their feelings and reactions to Jewish objects, artifacts, rituals, historical incidents and current events. A large number of artifacts is gathered and displayed at various places in the room on separate tables. One table perhaps would have a number of holiday rituals such as a Kippah, Tallit, or Havdala box, Shabbat candlesticks, a Siddur, a Pesach plate, etc. The second table could have some historical documents such as a newspaper clipping from the day Israel was born or the Six Day War or the like, a book about the Holocaust, a yellow arm band with a Jewish star, an anti-Semitic Russian pamphlet, etc. Still a third table might contain several emotionally charged objects such as a Catholic cross, a statue of a saint, a black mourners button, a copy of the Kaddish prayer, a copy of a birth announcement or a wedding announcement or Bar Mitzvah invitation and a Yahrzeit candle.

The group is divided into three groups and each group assigned to stand around, examine and look at the objects on the table. They then share their feelings with one another about the objects on the table. It is helpful to have an assistant facilitator present for each of the three small groups to keep the expressions focused on feeling rather than on the cognitive level. After approximately seven or eight minutes each group moves to a different table and repeats the process, and then to the third table.

The group then returns to their seats and writes down the following:

1. What was the strongest feeling evoked within me during this experience? Describe the object and the feeling around it.

2. Which object aroused the most pride within me? Name the object and describe in detail the feeling.

3. Which object aroused within me the greatest sadness? Name the object and describe in detail the feeling.

4. Which object aroused within me the greatest anger? Name the object and describe in detail the feeling.

Each person then finds a partner and each couple then finds another couple to make a group of four. Within that group of four each person will have a turn to speak individually with the other three.

Within each quartet two dyads are formed. The first topic of discussion is item number 1, the strongest feelings. Each person takes two minutes to share what he has written. At the conclusion of these four minutes each person finds a new partner within the quartet and discusses question number 2, feelings of pride. Then a third partner is found within the quartet and the feelings of sadness are discussed. Finally the whole quartet is reassembled and each person discusses his feelings of anger for one minute. Then the members of the quartet discuss how it was to share feelings, attitudes and values in distinction to most discussion groups which relate merely to the cognitive level.

The leader may then ask the group to make some "I learned...." statements or to discuss the whole exercise in terms of the opportunity to share feelings regarding Jewish rituals, historical experiences and personal reactions.

A variation of this exercise for a smaller group would be to have persons sit around in a circle and one at a time the facilitator passes around objects and has participants touch them, feel them, examine them and turn them around, hold them for a few minutes and then share a reaction. For example: A Tallit can be passed around and each person hold it for a minute, examine it and then express his feelings and pass it on, the next person doing the same thing. A second object to pass around the circle might be a picture of a Swastika. A third object might be a painting of an aged Jew studying Torah, etc., etc..

Developing Our Intuition

The leader prepares a tray on which he places ten small Jewish objects such as a paperback book, a Havadalah box, a Shabbat candlestick, a Mezuzah, a Jewish star, a small picture of some Jewish scene, a Kippah, etc. The tray and the objects on it are covered with a towel or sheet. The group is asked to sit quietly and make themselves very comfortable and relax. Perhaps a relaxation exercise such as tightening and loosening body muscles can be utilized.

The tray is brought into the room where the group is waiting. Each person is then asked to guess what Jewish objects might be on the tray. The leader tells participants to use their intuitive eye to guess what they think might be located on it. Each person is given pencil and paper and records ten things and then puts down the pencil and paper.

Participants are told that they will be given sixty seconds to look at the objects, and then will be asked to write down on the other side of the paper what they saw. The leader then removes the towel for a period of sixty seconds and everyone is permitted to look at the tray and to try and remember what the ten objects are. At that point participants are asked to turn the paper over, record the objects that they remember and put down the pencil and paper again.

The leader then removes the towel and each person compares his two lists with what is on the tray. The group is then asked to examine their intuitive style and see how good their guesses were.

No heavy explanations or interpretations are needed to process this exercise. It can be merely an act of enjoyment and an opportunity for some intuition development utilizing Jewish content objects. It is best to use this exercise in an on-going group in which the members feel comfortable with one another and in which there is a level of mutual acceptance. Only in this kind of atmosphere will people feel safe and comfortable enough to participate in such an unusual exercise. It would also best be utilized in a smaller group of from ten to twenty.

On Trial

The leader explains to the group that "We will now participate in a fantasy. Let us suppose that each person in this group is on trial in the Soviet Union for being a Jew. The crime of which you are accused is that you live a Jewish life. Your activities, your involvements, your commitments to Judaism and the Jewish people are a crime against the state."

Taking paper and pencil or pen, each person is then asked to compile a prosecutor's brief. In other words, each person will write a list of evidence which the prosecuting attorney can bring to convict that individual of being a Jew, of living a Jewish life. The evidence listed of course is not part of the fantasy, that is reality. It is based on the actual Jewish lifestyle of the person writing the list.

In other words, if the writer were on trial for being a Jew and were asked to compile evidence in the form of a prosecutor's brief, it would include some of the following: Attending Shabbat services, performing Sabbath rituals on Friday night, speaking in Hebrew to friends, reading Jewish books, participating in Soviet Jewry rallies, visiting the state of Israel three times, writing textbooks for Jewish educational purposes, etc., etc., etc.

Now each person will compile a brief of his own which the prosecuting attorney might use to convict you as a Jew. After fifteen or twenty minutes small groups of five or six are formed and each individual is asked to read the brief as evidence that he compiled. Another possibility is to ask the members of the small groups to decide "guilty" or "innocent" for each member. Criteria might be established in advance. Each person in the small group is then asked to complete the following sentence: One thing I could do in my life to give the prosecuting attorney a better case against me would be .... The leader then asks several members of the small group to share some of their sentences until some ten or fifteen are recited.

Favorite Jewish Ritual Objects

The group is divided into small groups of six. Each person in the smaller groups selects one Jewish ritual object. It may be something that he likes because of its esthetic appeal. Or it may be a ritual object which has special meaning to the person, such as a Tallit, or a Sukkah or Matzah. Each person in the group, after having selected these favorite Jewish ritual objects, tells the group what the object is and why he selected it.

The leader then tells the entire group that the next step is for that person to play a Gestalt awareness game by giving the ritual object a voice. Each person will speak as if he were that ritual object. For example, if one selected a Mezuzah, he might say: "I am a Mezuzah, I carry within me the aged and sacred words, "Shma Yisrael." I adorn the homes of every Jewish family. I am kissed frequently by people who pass through the doorway. I bear witness to the presence of a committed Jewish family. I have a beautiful case sometimes wooden, sometimes metal, frequently with beautiful decorations and art work. I am tiny but my significance goes far beyond my size. I am a constant reminder of Jewish obligations and privileges."

The leader asks if there are any questions to make sure everyone understands how this is to be done.

Each person is then asked to complete the following sentence. "One new thing I realize that attracts me to that ritual object is ...."

The group may then discuss their reactions to the exercise.

Designing a Jewish Flag

Materials required for this are crayons and/or magic markers and large sheets of paper, such as construction paper or newsprint. The leader begins by telling the story of how the Israeli flag came into existence. Prior to 1948 it was the flag of the World Zionist Movement.

We are fortunate in having a detailed description of how this flag came into existence. It was in 1905 and David Wolffsohn, successor to Theodore Herzl as President of the World Zionist Organization, was asked to create a flag for the Zionist Congress. These are the words of Mr. Wolffsohn: "At the request of our leader, Herzl, I came to Basle to make preparations for the Zionist Congress.... Among the many problems that occupied me then was one which contained something of the essence of the Jewish problem. What flag would we hang in the Congress Hall? Then an idea struck me. We have a flag-and it is blue and white. The Talit with which we wrap ourselves when we pray: that is our symbol. Let us take this Talit from its bag and unroll it before the eyes of Israel and the eyes of all nations. So I ordered a blue and white flag with the Shield of David painted upon it. That is how our national flag that flew over Congress Hall came into being. And no one expressed any surprise or asked whence it came or how".

Suppose you were David Wolffsohn and were asked to create a Jewish flag. What would it be like if you were to do it today, right now. What symbol or symbols would you select? What colors? What shapes, designs? What words, if any, would be included? What would be your idea of an ideal Jewish flag that would represent the aspirations of the Jewish people?

The leader then distributes the newsprint or construction paper and crayons and magic markers and gives the group approximately thirty to forty minutes to make a flag.

This activity can be processed in a manner similar to Activity 34 or 35. Namely, the group may parade around the room displaying their flags and then hang them on the wall. One by one each person can stand next to his flag and get reactions from the group, following which he elaborates on any symbolism that is still unexplained or uncovered.

The leader may then invite members of the group to think further on their own about the possible meanings that this flag might have regarding their own Jewish feelings and commitments.

ACTIVITY NUMBER 44

Jewish Values List

The leader distributes copies of the "Working List of Jewish Values" by Abraham Segal.

The leader explains that there is no one fixed set of Jewish values. Rather, many Rabbis, scholars and teachers have devised their own lists. Mr. Segal's list represents one tentative list which come out of his life-long pursuit of Jewish study.

The leader asks the group to study the list and to mark it in the following way: To place three stars next to those items on the list which the person feels have a great deal of significance for him personally. To place two stars next to those which the person feels are important. To place one star next to those which have some significance, but not a great deal, to that individual personally. The leader asks the group to divide into small groups of four. Within each quartet two dyads are formed and discuss with each other the following questions: Which one value in the entire list of thirty-two do you feel most strongly about? Each person takes two minutes of uninterrupted speaking time while the partner listens intently. At the end of that four minute period, new partners are formed within the same quartet and they then discuss the following questions: Which value do you feel least strongly about? At the end of that four minute period again new partners are found within the same quartet and the following question is discussed: Which one value in the list would you like to work on and improve in your own life?

At the end of these three dyadic interviews the leader may elicit reactions from the entire group. He might also wish to have the group make statements beginning with the words, "I learned....", "I discovered....", "I was surprised at....", "I became aware that....", "I re-learned that....".

WORKING LIST OF JEWISH VALUES

by Abraham Segal

1. Scholar and sage as the ideal Jewish character type.

2. Compassion toward all living things and the earth itself as expression of our love of God.

3. Sense of identification with all Jews, of heritage, rootedness, history, generation-binding ties.

4. Pleasure and enjoyment in Jewish living that embodies all the other values.

5. Mitzvot both obligations and opportunities: the "reward-in-itself."

6. God not a wonder-working magician, but man's partner, helper, teacher, guide.

7. Passionate zeal for study by all: reverent concentration on a few basic documents (Scripture): study as an essential form of prayer and service of God: vital importance of learning and knowledge.

8. Jewish practices in home and synagogue as expression of all other Jewish values.

9. Hebrew language as expression of all other Jewish values.

10. Covenant commitment of an entire people and their descendants forever to Jewish values.

11. Messianic ideals: world peace, brotherhood, freedom.

12. Social justice a major goal of human existence, a major criterion for human, national, communal, or personal salvation.

13. Worship and ceremonial not "communion" (sharing with God) but self-discovery, self-judgment, self-purposing, self-development.

14. Optimism in the struggle against the world's evil.

15. Importance of the group, the Jewish people, as source and target of individual effort.

16. Importance of the individual as well: his divine potential and divine obligation to achieve the very highest kind of human personality: his responsibility to himself.

17. The supreme value of life itself, above all other values except-- according to Jewish tradition--the still higher requirement of refusing to commit murder, adultery, or idolatry.

18. Sense of Jewish uniqueness, distinctiveness, difference, purpose and destiny.

19. Spiritual survival even more important than physical survival.

20. Family, school, synagogue, and community as vital agents for transmitting Jewish values from generation to generation.

21. Good citizenship plus strong and public Jewish life.

22. Obligation to support the state of Israel both as physical refuge and as cultural-spiritual center of Jewish living.

23. Jewish homeland as conditional, not guaranteed, but organically related to Jewish values as its chief purpose and vital prerequisities.

24. Rational, inquiring attitude toward life's problems.

25. Resistance to intermarriage and assimilation.

26. Resistance, physical and spiritual, to persecution.

27. Torah as continuing discovery (revelation) of God's guidance, demands, punishments, rewards.

28. Organic development in Jewish living achieved by continuing interaction of tradition, reinterpretation, and reform, in response to both external pressures and inner growth in understanding.

29. Basic harmony between reason and faith, science and religion, Judaism and the best in modern culture.

30. Ethics and morality as outcomes of religious search and religious faith.

31. Acceptance of difference and disagreement among Jews as part of a "family feeling" that also includes love, responsibility, pride, shame.

32. Our ability to grasp some measure of what God requires of us.

(Note: This is a "working" or tenative listing, not a definitive or exhaustive one. Order, numbering having no significance and are for reference purposes only.)

Creative Poetry

Each person has pencil or pen and paper and is told that this will be a creative writing exercise. There are two kinds of poems that can be written. Participants can write one or both.

The first is an acrostic poem. One word is selected as the theme of the poem and is then written vertically, each letter on a new line. For example the word Israel would be written:

I _____
S _____
R _____
A _____
E _____
L _____

The poem would then be written with each of these letters beginning that particular line. For example the first line would begin with I, the second line with an S, the third line with an R and so on. The following acrostic poem will illustrate.

Love treats
Others as if they were of more
Value than
Even our own life.

The second kind of poem is called by the French word Cinquain pronounced sin-can).

Line one: The title (a one word noun).
Line two: Describe the title word in two adjectives.
Line three: Three words describing the noun, the first
               of which ends in "ing".
Line four: A four word phrase describing a feeling
               about the noun.
Line five: A one word synonym for the noun.

The following Cinquain is an example of this kind of poetry.

God
Compassionate, forgiving
Acting for human kind
Always willing to forget
Love

The leader then asks each individual to find someone in the group that he knows least well to share his poetic creations. The leader may then ask a few people who were particularily impressed with hearing their partner's poem, to read it to the entire group (with the partner's permission).

Some or all of these poems may be posted on the wall or bulletin board, or printed in the group newspaper.

What's Your Button?

Each person receives a pen or pencil and paper. The leader explains that many people wear buttons on their chest to display some point of view or advocate some political candidate. This exercise will draw upon our creativity to create some buttons expressing opinions and attitudes of our own on Jewish issues of concern to us. The group is asked to quot some buttons they have seen recently.

The leader may select a specific area for which the buttons should be created, such as the Jews in the U.S.S.R., or the political situation in the Middle East, or some other current political, cultural, social or ethical issue. Or the leader may leave the choice of subject area completely open-ended.

The leader then draws on the chalkboard or flip chart six or eight button shapes such as circles, squares, triangles, oblongs, etc. Each participant can copy these six or eight shapes and is instructed to write in each one some slogan, word or phrase expressing a position which he holds. The leader should encourage the participants to think carefully about the issues that they feel most strongly about and to create meaningful buttons on their sheet of paper.

After five or six minutes, when the participants have completed their buttons, the leader asks the group to prioritize the six or eight buttons writing No. 1 by the side of the one most important to him, No. 2 next to the second most important, and so on. Groups of four are then formed and each person displays and explains his buttons and the priorities he attaches to them.

The next step is for each person to cut out one of the buttons and pin or tape it to his chest. Participants then mill around the room reading each others buttons. The group then returns to the small groups of four and deals with the following questions one at a time:

How do you expect people to react to your button?
Is there some place that you would never wear your button?
Is there some place that you would be afraid to wear your button?

After these issues are dealt with each person should make a new button that he would never wear. After this button is made, each person in the quartet shows the button and the reason why he would never wear it. Each person then asks regarding the same button he would never wear:

Who do you think would give you the most trouble with that button?

Another possible question for the small groups is: What things can you do to help bring about the condition which you advocate in the original series of buttons to which you give the highest priorities?

I learned this activity from Robert Bolton

Jewish Identity Rank Orders

The Rank Order exercise is one of the staples of Value Clarification. The Jewish identity rank orders all deal with some aspect of being Jewish.

The leader distributes the Jewish Identity Rank Orders sheet and instructs each individual to rank his choices, that is, prioritize the list of choices found on the sheet. It is always helpful to explain when giving a rank order that No. 1 is the highest or first choice, No. 2 the second choice, and so on. People frequently find it confusing in the process of numbering their selections.

When it looks as though most people have completed ranking on their sheets, the leader may ask for a show of hands as follows:

Who selected American as their first choice in their first rank order?
Who selected Jew?
Human being?
Male/female?

The leader then asks several persons who selected American as first choice and to comment on their selection. The same is done for the following three categories until each category has been "defended" by two or three participants. The same procedure is then followed for each of the other Rank Orders.

Participants are then asked to write on the other side of the piece of paper a list of ten priorities that they think are necessary for creative Jewish survival, for a creative Jewish community.

A number of participants can then read their lists and a general discussion on the future of the American Jewish Community can then follow.

JEWISH IDENTITY RANK ORDERS

1) Rank the following roles in the order in which they play the most significant part in your life:

_____ American
_____ Jew
_____ human being
_____ male/female

2) Which holiday plays the most important role in preserving Jewish identity?

_____ Pesach
_____ Hanukkah
_____ Shabbat
_____ Israel Independence Day

3) Which of the following persons contributed most to Jewish community life in America?

_____ David Ben Gurion
_____ Mordecai M. Kaplan
_____ Martin Buber
_____ Golda Meir
_____ Moshe Dayan
_____ Chaim Potok

4) If we were forced to select only one institution to save in American Jewry, which would it be?

_____ the synagogue
_____ the Jewish Community Center
_____ Jewish Community Federation
_____ Hebrew days schools, (K-12)

Being a Jewish Parent

Each person receives pen or pencil and a copy of the Rank Orders on being a Jewish parent.

The leader distributes copies of the Rank Orders and asks each person to rank the choices in the order of their preference. One possible way to process this exercise is the same as in the previous one, asking a number of individuals who selected each choice as their first to explain their selections.

Another interesting possibility is to have each person find a partner and discuss Rank Order No. 1, and than a new partner for No. 2, and so on, so that each person will have discussed these rank orders with five others in the room. That enables each participant to share opinions with different kinds of individuals.

A good way to conclude this exercise is by having each person write on 3 x 5 cards a number of "I learned...." statements. These may begin with, "I learned that I....", "I was surprised that I....", "I relearned that I....", "I discovered that I....".

RANK ORDERS ON "BEING A JEWISH PARENT"

1)   Which is worst: If your child:

       a)   married an unconverted non-Jew
       b)   converted to Hare Krishna
       c)   was jailed for selling hard drugs

2)   Which role is more prominent in your life?

       a)   human being
       b)   husband/wife
       c)   parent
       d)   Jew

3)   Which do you want most for your child?

       a)   high income
       b)   good health
       c)   graduate level education
       d)   personal happiness
       e)   lead an active Jewish life

4)   Which contributes most to Jewish family life?

       a)   attending Shabbat services together
       b)   Shabbat nite (Friday nite) meal together
       c)   open communication
       d)   mutual acceptance

5)   Which has the greatest influence on the life of a teenager today?

       a)   home
       b)   synagogue
       c)   public school
       d)   peer group
       e)   TV

Statements on Jewish Parenting

Each person should have pen or pencil and a copy of the Statements on Jewish Parenting.

On the reverse side of the sheet of paper each person writes a personal reaction to each of the five quotations. These reactions should be divided into two parts:

a)   What I think this statement means.
      (a conceptual explanation)

b)   A personal example from my own life or from that of someone
      I know that illustrates the point being made in this quotation.

Groups of four are then formed and from the group of four two dyats are formed.   These dyads then discuss their reactions to statement No. 1. After each person has had two minutes to share his reaction, each person finds a new partner within the same quartet and either discusses quotation No. 2 or No. 3, whichever they select.   After that four minute sequence each person finds a new partner within the same quartet and discusses reactions to either quotation No. 4 or No. 5.

Each person then writes the following sentence: "To me the most important thing about being a Jewish parent is...".

The quartet reassembles and each person reads his sentence. After all four persons have read their sentences group members within the quartet may ask each other questions and continue the discussion.

The leader may then call on one representative from each quartet, and ask for a brief summary of the highlights of the discussion.

STATEMENTS ON JEWISH PARENTING

1) "Man cannot exist without woman, nor woman without man; nor both without Shekhinah (Divine Presence)" Genesis Rabbah 8:9 (Midrash)

2) "Better a morsel of dry bread with peace than a house full of feasting with strife." Proverbs 17:1.

3) "Happy is the generation when elders listen to the young; then, the young will listen to their elders." Talmud, Rosh Hashanah 25b.

4) Hasidic Tale: A parent tells the Rabbi he is having difficulty with his son and asks what to do. Rabbi: "Love him more than ever."

5) "God did not make woman from man's head that she should not be ruled by him; nor from his feet that she should not be his slave; but from his side that she should be near his heart." Midrash, Gen. Rabbah 18:2.

Tomorrow Morning's Headline

This is a fantasy exercise. It should be used by someone who has done fantasy before and knows some of the general principles involved. It is also better used with a group that has met before, rather than doing this kind of deep exercise at the early stage of a group's work.

Participants are asked to find a comfortable position sitting or lying. If possible, lights may be dimmed. The leader asks the group to relax and let the tension flow out of their body so that they are in the optimum psychological position for an effective guided fantasy. The leader says something like the following to the group:

"Please close your eyes and feel yourself become completely relaxed. Let the tension flow out of your body. See if there are any tight spots and let the tightness go and become more and more relaxed.

"Before your eyes you see tomorrow morning's newspaper. You are looking at the headline. The headline of tomorrow morning's newspaper has an important announcement that will directly effect the future of the Jewish people. You are looking at the headline and as you look letters fall into place. Letters become words and the words form an important piece of news for world Jewry. See what letters and words fall into place in the newspaper headline. See what your newspaper says, which you see in front of your eyes."

The leader now allows several minutes to pass while the participants complete the guided fantasy. The leader then says:

"Whenever you are ready open your eyes and slowly come back to this room again."

At that point the lights are turned up, if they were dimmed, and the leader asks several people to tell what was in their headline. In a group of fifteen or twenty it is possible to hear the headline of everyone who is willing to share what he saw.

The leader may then ask the group if anyone notices any patterns among the various headlines. There will probably be some notice that a great many of the fantasies dealt with Israel and the Middle East. Another person might point out that many or perhaps even most of the headlines have very pessimistic and disastrous quality. Some discussion on Jewish fears and insecurities might now take place. It is worthwhile to point out that because of past years of persecution, anti-semitism, and present difficulties in the U.S.S.R., with Jews in Arab countries, and the difficulties in the Middle East, the Jews are very naturally fearful about the status of their fellow Jews. Anyone not taking into consideration the real and very deep fears and insecurities of the contempory Jew is not fully aware of that significant dimension of modern Jewish living.

Other significant patterns and/or ideas that emerge from these fantasies can also be commented upon and discussed. This exercise generally produces very rich material for discussion and exploration.

Right Now I'm Feeling....

This exercise should be used only by a skilled group leader. It has potential for reaching very deeply into the soul of the participants and for facilitating close human contact between the members of the group when used properly.

Each person should be given a copy of the "Right Now I'm Feeling" sheet and be instructed to make a mark on the continuum most closely resembling his present state of feeling on each of the first six issues. Dr. Sidney Simon refers to what he calls "compulsive moderates" who constantly choose the exact middle of every continuum. The leader should encourage members of the group not to select the exact middle because in most cases that is really hiding their true feelings.

When the leader sees that most people have completed marking each of the six continuums, the group is ready for the next step. The group divides itself into small groups of three persons. Each person in the group of three talks for two minutes about the first continuum, "myself". Then each participant shares the place on the continuum that he marked with the description of his feelings about the future. Then a new group of three is formed so that each person has two new partners and the same process is repeated for No. 3 and No. 4. After that sequence a third triad is formed and continuums No. 5 and No. 6 are discussed.

At that point the leader may decide that he does not want to utilize the 7th, 8th, and 9th continuums and may merely move on to another activity or other part of the program. Should the leader decide that the group is at a level of emotional readiness and a level of warmth and mutual acceptance to explore their feelings more deeply, he may continue with discussing questions 7, 8, and 9. These last three should be done in the same triad so that a sense of trust can build and people feel free to risk. In fact, participants should be asked to form a triad among persons in the group whom they know best and with whom they feel at home and comfortable.

At the end of this exercise the leader should ask for any unfinished business, any further comments or questions, and finally a number of individuals may volunteer to share their actions to the entire activity.

Since this exercise involves deep feelings, it should not be rushed, and the leader should make sure that no one is left hanging without the opportunity to fully express and deal with these deep feelings.

49

Right Now I'm Feeling....

1) About myself
   Sort of - "eh" _____ Super

2) About my future
   Concerned _____ Charged up

3) About my job (school)
   Bad news _____ fantastic

4) About my faith
   Apathetic _____ freaked out

5) About being Jewish
   Could care less _____ totally committed

6) About Israel
   So what? _____ rabid Zionist

- - - - - -

Going deeper....

7) About my marriage (or other significant relationship)
   At a low point _____ renewed & excited

8) About my death
   Frightened _____ ready whenever it happens

9) About my masculinity/femininity
   Totally inadequate _____ the best I've been

Values Sheets

Values Sheets can be designed by a creative group leader by taking a brief quotation, a sentence or a paragraph and adding a number of questions below.

The first question or two should relate to the specific content of the material quoted, to understand what the author had in mind. The second and third should relate more to the conceptual level and extract some of the principles involved in material quoted. The fifth and sixth questions should be more personalized. They should relate the material directly to the life of the participants so that he feels as though this quotation was written directly for him or relating to him.

The general way to process Values Sheets is to have individuals answer the questions either in their mind or in writing, then forming small groups to share their answers.

The leader may then call on a representative of some of the small groups for a brief summary of the major points of the discussion.

Values Sheets are used to enhance programs and classroom discussion relating to a specific theme. The quotation used to spark the questions and discussion should be one that is controversial, strongly stated, perhaps inspiring or otherwise lending itself to meaty discussion.

On the pages that follow there are several samples of Values Sheets created and utilized by the author.

VALUES SHEET # 11

Dr. Dov Peretz Elkins
GROWTH ASSOCIATES
Box 8429, Rochester, NY 14618
716-244-1225

Jewish Pulse on Eve of '77

Jewish Adv.
12-30-76

US Jewish Family Under Pressure

By RICHARD YAFFE

NEW YORK (JCNS) — Barring a major upheaval in the American economy, the Jewish community should be able to maintain its above - average position on the socio economic scale, according to Dr. Eli Ginzberg, considered the country's leading man-power expert.

Dr. Ginzberg, the Burton Hepburn professor of economics at Columbia University and chairman of the National Commission for Manpower Policy, told the American Jewish Committee's National Executive Council in Dallas that the prospects for a stable economy are good and that Jews would benefit from a continuing decline in discrimination based on religion.

There are several sociological "ifs" that could mitigate against the continued prosperity of the Jews, he said. Among these is the "current oversupply of college - trained people" which, he said, would "slow the progress of many young Jews now entering the labor force."

He also noted that the rapid growth of the South and Southwest, "with their relatively sparse Jewish populations, and the retardation in the rate of growth in the North, where most Jews are concentrated," could act as deterrents to further economic improvement of the Jews."

Dr. Ginzberg noted that the Orthodox Jewish community was one "whose practices inhibit their occupational advance because they shun secular colleges and are disinclined to have their women work."

Mervin H. Riseman, chairman of the AJC's Jewish Commual Affairs Commission, reported that the Jewish family, traditionally a stronghold of warmth and togetherness and a major factor in the transmission of Jewish values, identity and continuity, is "beset by ten problems that could lead to the attrition of the Jewish community."

See FAMILY
(Continued on Page 20)

(Continued from Front Page)

1. "More Jews marry later than members of other groups.

2. "Most Jewish singles groups no longer operate solely for the purpose of 'matching.' These groups are now supportive of singles and the single way of life.

3. "The divorce rate is rising. There appears to be no stigma for the failure of marriage and there is no presumption of permanence.

4. "The birthrate is falling and childlessness has become socially acceptable.

5. "Financial success rather than the rearing of children has become for many the major goal of the family.

6. "The degree and intensity of family interaction has decreased, although it continues to be higher than that of other religious and ethnic groups.

7. "There is less socializing across generational lines, partly as a result of geographical mobility.

8. "The sense of responsibility of individual family members to other family members has decreased.

9. "The rule of Jewishness is no longer central to the lives of many individual family members.

10. "Intermarriage has resulted in a lessening of involvement of the Jewish partner in Jewish life and less emphasis on the Jewish aspects of family events."

Riseman's report was in the nature to a prelude to the announcement of a three - year study by his committee under the heading "Jewish Concern about Family Life." This will examine the ways that changing family patterns in society at large are affecting Jewish families, and the consequent effect on the transmission of Jewish values and identity to children.

The project, in addition to considering the ten problems besetting the family will consider federal and state laws, public policies and Jewish communal services in terms of their impact on the family. The study will be conducted simultaneously at the national regional and local levels.

Questions to Think on & talk about:

1) Which of the ten problems of the Jewish family do you think is most serious?
2) With which do you have most personal experience?
3) If you could change one of them tomorrow, at will, which would it be? Explain.
4) What is meant by the "rule of Jewishness" in #9? Is it central in the life of your family?
5) Do you agree with #6? Does it reflect your own experience with Jewish families you are familiar with?
6) What could you do, personally, to reverse the national trend toward the disintegration of the Jewish family & therefore the attrition of the Jewish community?
7) Any other thoughts about this article & its message?

(From Life Is For Living, by Saul Teplitz, Jonathan David Publishers pp. 66-7.)

"There was once a scottie dog who found himself lost and alone in a neighborhood of Irish terriers. Every time the scottie walked down the street, the terriers would bark at him in rage. He was quite puzzled and hurt, but instead of wondering what bothered the terriers, he began to analyze himself. Perhaps the terriers barked at him because he was different. He, therefore, tried very hard to be like the terriers. He began to wag his tail as they did and to prick up his ears as they did. He even barked in as perfect an imitation as could be achieved. And still they barked every time he went by.

"The scottie then decided to call in experts to write scholarly dissertations which would prove the greatness of the contributions of the scotties to canine civilization. Soon there were mountains of statistics to point up the courage of the scotties through a computation of the number of people they had rescued from burning buildings and drownings. Unfortunately, the only ones that read the books and the statistics were other scotties. Whatever the scottie did to impress or to imitate left the terriers unmoved. They continued to bark as in the past. Finally, the scottie decided that since he was a scottie, he had better act like one and live like one, and be the best possible scottie he could be. And if the terriers still barked, there was nothing he could do about it."

1. What is this all about?

2. In what situations do you feel like the scottie?

3. What emotions and thoughts do you have when in these situations? What happens to these?

4. In what ways do you pretend to be something you are not so you will be accepted?

5. To whom are you a terrier?

6. What do you get out of not accepting or putting down others?

7. What are some things you have to work on regarding accepting yourself and accepting others?

8. Do you agree or disagree with the last sentence?

COURAGE: What it is? Do you have it? Where do you get it?

We are capable at the same time of taking risks and of estimating them before-hand. Others are brave out of ignorance. When they stop to think they begin to fear. But the man who most truly can be accounted brave is he who most knows the meaning of what is sweet in life and what is terrible, then goes out undeterred to meet what is to come.   SOCRATES

James B. Conant, President of Harvard University, kept among other objects on his desk a little model of a turtle, under which was the inscription,"Consider the turtle. He makes progress only when he sticks his neck out."

No one ever moves forward with head in a shell.

"He who loses wealth loses much. He who loses a friend loses more. But he who loses courage loses all."   CERVANTS

"A Commander-in-Chief received a message telling him that his main line of defense had been broken by the enemy. He was greatly distressed and his emotions showed plainly on his countenance. His wife heard the nature of the message, and entering her husband's room, she said: 'I too at this very moment have received tidings worse than yours.' 'And what are they?' inquired the Commander with agitation. 'I have read discouragement on your face,' replied the wife. 'Loss of courage is worse than loss of defense.'"

(Talmudic Anthology, ed. Louis Newman, quoted in Gittelsohn, CONSECRATED UNTO ME)

"Who is courageous? He who masters his passions."
                              Ethics of the Fathers, Talmud

Questions to write on and to think on:

1. Tell of two times in your life where you displayed enormous courage. (Define it for yourself. You don't have to belittle your courage. If it felt coura-geous, especially at that time, tell us about it.)

2. What are some things you've seen others do which you would consider courageous. Make a catalog of courageous acts you have known about for all of us to consider.

3. O.K. Here is the real question. What are some things you need to do right now in your life which will take courage?

4. When do you want to get started? How do you want to get started? How can we help you.

GROWTH ASSOCIATES - Human Relations Consultants and Publishers
Box 8429
Rochester, New York 14618
(716) 244-1225

Friday, July 1, 1977 Page 6

MAX LERNER

Spooky Spiritual Scene

LOS ANGELES — Do you believe that a man or a woman — or a group of them — can bring a spook into being, by sheer mental concentration? Or that a spook can materialize and dematerialize in a room, becoming a guide and adviser, watching over his charge?

I have just attended one of those annual conferences where you spend a long weekend at countless workshops, half-listen to a list of speakers, and scribble endless notes to yourself which you proceed to lose. This time it was a meeting of the Assn. for Humanistic Psychology.

I came to it to speak but remained to listen, and to keep track of some new trends in the psychological disciplines.

One speaker who had a great impact on her listeners was Elizabeth Kubler-Ross, author of "On Death and Dying." While she talked of her work with the dying, to help them and their families to accept the fact of death, her more explosive theme was her experience with several being she called her "spooks."

One of them is an entity who materializes at sessions she holds regularly with a large therapy group, who talks, sings, answers questions — and dematerializes. Another is her own personal spook, or "guide," who turns up at odd times, in odd places, and shows his concern for her by giving her advice about her life.

The experience with ghosts and spooks out of the spirit world is not new. It has been part of the spiritualist scene for centuries, and has excited discussion which has never resolved the question of whether it is valid or the result of deception and self-deception.

What is new is the entrance of someone like Kubler-Ross into the area of psychic phenomena, with her solid learning, her professional prestige and the quiet but earnest self-assurance which gives her considerable credibility.

"As a psychoanalyst," she tells her audience, "I have had to deal with the reality principle for years. Yet here I am talking of my spooks." It is a disarming bit of self-scrutiny.

Kubler-Ross has nevertheless not escaped a heavy barrage of professional criticism, from psychiatrists and psychologists. They were impressed with her work on dying. But when she reaches out to the farther shores beyond sensory experience, she has heavy sailing with her colleagues.

Some of them suggest that having worked so long on death, with empathy and compassion, she developed a deeply felt need to believe in the spirit world beyond the senses.

She is obviously aware of the criticism. She tells how her "guide" has warned her that she will be "shredded to pieces. Yet she has evidently decided to be increasingly open about her experiences and her statements and discussions at professional meetings. It takes courage.

I have tried to put together, from several sources, a picture of what actually happens in the private sessions that Kubler-Ross leads, including a group of about 175 who meet weekly at Escondido, in Southern California.

The "being" or "entity" who materializes seems to change height and bulk from appearance to appearance, yet presumably he is recognizable each time. He speaks, jokes, sings. During her Los Angeles talk Kubler-Ross played what she described as a record of his voice as he joined a member of the group in singing "You are my sunshine, my only sunshine." This everyday, even trivial, activity seems to be characteristic of the world of psychic phenomena.

One could dismiss all this as old, weary stuff, especially when it crops up again in California, which has been the happy hunting ground of mediums, ghosts and spooks.

Yet two things must give us some pause. One is that parapsychology and transpersonal psychology have become recognized disciplines in recent years, the former having been admitted to the American Assn. for the Advancement of Science, with an impressive group of sponsors.

The other is the spread of interest and awareness about the transpersonal among laymen throughout the nation, which has come partly out of recent brain research, partly out of the decay of religious faith and the need for something to replace it. We are in an era very similar to that of American thought in the days of Emerson, who believed in an "oversoul."

Today we call it a pervasive energy field which wraps the cosmos in a vast cocoon of consciousness. In Emerson's day they spoke of "transcendentalism." Today we speak of a "separate reality."

Do I believe it? I am skeptical, but I don't dismiss it by completely disbelieving it. I maintain what Coleridge called a "willing suspension of disbelief," which leaves me open to whatever emerges from the efforts to test and validate the kind of experience Kubler-Ross describes.

Saul Bellow, in his Nobel Prize talk and in a recent essay, has urged writers to talk about this. He is worth heeding.

QUESTIONS TO WRITE AND THINK ON:

1) What have you read about parapsychology & transpersonal psychology?
   Can you define them?
2) Do you know anyone who has had psychic experiences?
3) Have you ever had any?
4) On a continuum of one to ten, where would you place your
   belief level in these phenomena?
5) What value do they have for people? For you? What dangers?
6) Other comments....

Values Sheet
Dr. Dov Peretz Elkins
GROWTH ASSOCIATES
Box 8429
Rochester, NY 14618

Brainstorming a Concept

The same principles of brainstorming described in Activity Number 8 in the previous volume, <u>Clarifying Jewish Values</u>, apply here as well. Namely, (1) the goal is for a large quantity of ideas, (2) no evaluation should be made until the brainstorming phase is completed, (3) the wilder the idea is the better, and (4) "piggybacking" or modifying and adapting ideas and adding to the total number of suggestions is encouraged.

The technique of brainstorming is applied in this activity to a specific Hebrew or Judaic concept. For example the group may brainstorm definitions and synonyms for the word Shalom. The leader would write on the chalkboard or flip chart as the members of the group call out their ideas. Since ideas come very quickly during such a brainstorming session, the leader should not be concerned about facing the group or calling on individuals, but rather just standing at the chalkboard and writing as fast as he can. Should there be a lull in the brainstorming then the leader may turn around and face the group and say, "Who else has an idea of a snyonym or definition of the word Shalom?". Groups have been known to generate fifty to a hundred such snyonyms and/or definitions. These enable the group to share their understanding of the ideas and to offer an expanded version of the original concept. The material generated by this brainstorming activity can then be used for other activities such as creative writing, drawing, discussion of philosophic and ideological issues and so forth.

Some other concept words which might be the focus of a brainstorm activity are:

God

Torah

Bible (Tanakh)

Talmud

Tzedaka

Zedek

Mishpacha

Am Yisrael

. . . .

. . . .

Hum a Hebrew Song

This exercise can be used effectively only with a group of persons which has some familiarity with at least a small number of Hebrew songs.

The goal is to help participants reach into some of the deeper levels of their consciousness in order to surface Jewish issues with which they are dealing in their present life.

The leader asks participants to begin with humming when he gives the signal, just to make a noise or sound, without concern as to what it sounds like. They will then gradually let the hum turn into a melody, a Hebrew or Jewish melody with which they are familiar. They continue humming their melody until it soon becomes recognizable.

The leader now asks the group members to relate the words or meaning of the song that came to their mind to some Jewish issue or to some Jewish concern relating to their personal lives. For example: If one were to sing Hava Nagila, the person might be seeking in his life to find more joy and happiness in Jewish celebrations. Or, to the contrary, the person might be trying to emerge from a period of depression or sadness relating to the loss of a loved one and want to emerge from that period of mourning into a more joyful existence. A song relating to Israel such as Hatikvah, might say something to the person regarding his desire to travel to Israel or some other aspect of his relationship with the State of Israel. It is best not to give too many examples to the group but rather let them come up with whatever interpretation suggests itself in their minds. The main thing is to address the question to the group: What relationship is there between that song, its words, its melody, its meaning and some Jewish issues with which you are dealing in your present life?

The leader then gives members of the group a moment or so to come up with that interpretation. He then calls upon several people, as many as possible, to make the connection between the song they were humming and the issue relating to it. If the group is not too large, everyone should be given an opportunity to describe whatever thoughts came into his mind.

I learned this activity from Will Schutz.

57

Problem Solving Groups

Problem solving groups are an effective way of generating creative solutions to significant Jewish problems.

The exercise has five basic steps:

1. Posing the problem
2. The leader suggests two alternative solutions
3. The group brainstorms additional alternative solutions
4. Independent thinking: action decision
5. Sharing

The first step is to pose the problem. For example, the leader says, "We are going to discuss a certain problem using the strategy of Problem Solving Groups. The problem we will deal with is how can we get Jews to know more about their heritage?"

The second step involves the leader presenting two possible solutions. Two suggestions in this case might be: 1) Levy a voluntary tax on all Jews in a community for Jewish education for adults and children.

2) Provide more subsidies to Hebrew teacher training colleges to help attract more qualified students.

Step 3 involves the group then using their own creative solutions after having heard two possibilities from the leader. The leader's suggestions act as priming the pump. Follow the standard procedures for brainstorming; namely, the more ideas the better, the wilder the ideas the better, and no evaluation during the ideas-generating stage.

The fourth step is for each individual to look over the long list of solutions generated through the brainstorming procedure and to select one or two or three which will become "action decisions." These will be the things that the individual selects from the list to put into action for himself.

The fifth and last step is for each participant to share the decisions that he has made regarding his own involvement in that issue. This can be done in a whole group or in smaller groups. Perhaps a self-contract might be utilized during this step (Activity No. 25). The basic idea is to move from insight to action, from idea to commitment.

I learned this exercise from Merrill Harmin.

Role Reversals

The role reversal is a very effective technique for helping people see and understand on a deep level the position of those with whom they strongly disagree.

The basic procedure is very simple. A discussion is held between two individuals or two groups of individuals on a controversial subject. The difference is that each individual in the discussion plays the opposite role of his own. For example: In the group of parents and children, the children would take the position of the parent and the parent the stance of the children. One subject of debate might be for example the question of intermarriage or interdating. In a role reversal discussion the children acting the role of the parent would take the position of arguing against interdating. The parent, taking the role of the child, would argue in favor of interdating or inter-marriage. (A full description of exactly this program is given in the author's book, Humanizing Jewish Life, pages 131-139).

Another possible discussion would be between an Arab and a Jew, the Jew taking the position of the Arab and vice versa. A third possibility would be a debate between a Jew and a Christian, each taking an opposing position. The Arab and the Jew, for example, might debate some issue of importance in the Middle East such as the role of the Palestinians, the giving up of occupied territory, etc. The Jew and the Christian might debate the significance of the New Testament, the place of Jesus and Judaism in Christianity, the role of modern Christians in Middle Eastern politics, etc.

In the event that there are no people present who hold an opposite point of view such as a parent, Arab or a Christian, group members can role play these positions and argue from the assumed point of view of such as opposing debater and other group members can take their own side of the question.

Role reversals can be enormously effective in getting persons to see the point of view with which they strongly disagree. So often emotional overtones cloud the thinking of individuals when they are involved personally in important issues. Being required to marshal arguments in favor of the other point of view requires the individual to get into the skin and empathize with the other individual and see at least some of the truth of the other side.

Sufficient time should be allowed at the conclusion of the exercise to permit those individuals who assumed roles opposite their own to fully de-role. In other words to share fully the feeling they had as they were taking the position opposite their own and what the whole experience did for them as a person.

Group Fantasy Story

This is a fun activity, one of a lighter variety. The group makes up a story by having each person add a sentence to the progress of the narrative. The facilitator starts by giving one or two sentences and then signaling to a member of the group to add a second sentence and then the story continues as each person in order around the group adds to the story. Participants should be sitting in a circle and told in advance who will be called on first and after that the story will move around the circle to the right after the first person.

Some sample beginnings might be:

The president of the United States called a special meeting with ten leading American Rabbis....

A new instutition in Jewish life appeared in 1980....

King Hussein and the Israeli Prime Minister sat down and initialed the document....

Coming off the plane at Ben Gurion airport was one of the most significant people who ever visited Israel....

The members of our congregation were presented an extraordinarily unique reward by the Israeli army at the top of Masada....

Three American youngsters, age thirteen years, were singled out by the government of Israel for their heroism and bravery....

The meeting between Golda Meir and Elizabeth Taylor was an extremely fascinationg one. The two Jewish mothers spoke about....

Note: The leader can intervene at any point in the story to add more flavor and/or humor by changing locations, adding characters, or thickening the plot in any other way.

No processing is necessary.

A Prayer For A Speedy Recovery

This is a prayer-exercise for an on-going group.   It is a good example of how some of the modern human potential techniques can be combined with traditional Jewish religious practices.

If a member of the group is ill, the group can perform their prayer-exercise.   Members of the group are instructed to rub their palms together. This has the effect of bringing energy into the hands.   Members of the group then hold their hands up, palms facing away and begin to chant "Shalom." As members are holding their palms up and chanting Shalom, they may close their eyes and concentrate on the person who is ill and send energy to that person from their hands and from their voice.   As the word Shalom is being chanted the second syllable is held for a long period of time and repeated several times, during which a member of the group may read the traditional get-well prayer Mee She-Bayrach.

This exercise of rubbing palms and sending energy through the hands and voice may also be directed toward a member of the group who is in need of special love or attention or healing energy of the group.   In such a case instead of the get-well prayer in Hebrew, another similar Mee She-Bayrach may be used.

It is an interesting historical footnote to realize that the ancient priests (Kohanim) would also raise their hands, palms facing away as they blessed the people.   During this exercise participants may wish to hold their fingers to make the letter Shin as did the ancient Kohanim. The letter Shin stands for the Hebrew word Shaddai, which means "Almighty." This is done by holding the hands in the following position: The second and third fingers are joined together and the fourth and fifth are joined together thus making, with the thumb, three prongs of the letter Shin. In this way members of the group send the focus person not only their own energy, but healing energy of the universe and that of the Almighty as well.

Adapted from Meditation for Children by Debra Rozman (Millbrae, CA: Celestial Arts, 1976, Page 137).

An Experience of Isolation

This can be a very risky exercise and should be performed with upmost caution by a skilled and trained facilitator. The purpose of the experience is to create a simulation in which the individuals involved feel directly the pain and anxiety of prejudice and discrimination.

The group is divided into small groups of six. The first step is to have each person say a few words about himself so that the group begins to become acquainted one with another. The second step is to select one quality or characteristic which is possessed by only one member of the group. For example: One person may have red hair. Or all members of the group but one might be wearing loafers. Or all may be boys but one girl. They all may live in one area of the community and the other person in another area. The idea is to search for one person in the group who is in some way different from the other members of the group. This should not be "different" because of any negative characteristic. This will prevent the exercise from becoming highly charged with authentic anger and hatred. And at the same time it will permit the experience nevertheless to be fully felt.

The group is told that the one person in each small group who is selected as being in some way different from the other members of the group, is to leave the group and go to a designated space in the room. All of the eliminated persons will join together in their own small group in this designated portion of the room.

The group is told in the hearing of those eliminated that they are now to discuss their opinions about the person who has been sent away and to try to look for mostly negative things though keeping the atmosphere some-what light and not unduly negative. In other words not to go into any heavy critical matters but just talk about some minor aspects of that person which might have an irritating effect on others.

After three or four minutes the leader then asks the members of the small groups as well as the group of eliminated persons to share their feelings about what has taken place.

At that point the group of eliminated persons is focused upon and these persons are asked to share their feelings with the entire group. In all likelihood they will express feelings of isolation, rejection, anger, resentment, indignation, hurt and so on. The leader may then ask for the feelings of several other members who participated in the process of eliminating a group member. The entire group may then focus on the conceptual question on what it feels like to be a member of a minority group and what it feels like to be rejected and discriminated against. If the exercise worked effectively, there should be much data produced to help participants understand on a feeling level the problems of prejudice and discrimination in our society.

In order to restore good feelings among members of the group it is wise at this point to make some positive gesture of reconciliation such as one of the following:

a) Have the eliminated member return to the group, lie on his stomach and get a group message.

b) Have the person lie on his back and be lifted quietly by the members of the group as they sway him and hum gently.

Other possible validation exercises can be found in the author's Teaching People To Love Themselves, pages 250-265. (An especially effective technique is the Car Wash, found on page 254.)

Organizational Strengths and Weaknesses

The leader explains that the goals of this exercise will be to express the strengths and weaknesses of the organization, to help determine the feasibility of its goals, to develop a realistic pride in the group and to locate areas for improvement. Each person should have pen or pencil and paper. The leader instructs the group to take fifteen minutes to list all the strengths and weaknesses of the organization listing at least five of each.

The leader then writes on chalkboard or flip chart a combined list so that a large number of strengths and weaknesses are written in front of the group. Duplications should be eliminated.

The next step is for each person to look at the master list and write the ten most important strengths and ten most important weaknesses in his opinion.

Following this the group breaks into small groups of four and creates a group rank order of the ten most significant strengths and ten most significant weaknesses through a consensual process.

The final step is for the entire group to reconvene and to create one list of strengths and weaknesses through the process of voting. The ten items which receive the largest number of votes will be those that the group might want to consider in some further way. That is, to greater develop the strengths and to attempt to eliminate some of the weaknesses.

A general discussion of future strengths may now take place.

Adapted from Educational Change: A Humanistic Approach, edited by Ray Eiben and Al Milliren (La Jolla, CA: University Associates, 1976) Pages 144-145.

Confessional

This activity and the next two that follow are designed to be specifically performed around the time of Jewish holidays. The Confessional is a High Holy Day exercise. A pencil or pen and a paper are required for this exercise.

The leader distributes copies of the Confessional from the Yom Kippur liturgy, Ashamnu. The leader explains that this is a common, well-known confessional prayer from the High Holy Day Mahzor. He points out that the original Hebrew is constructed so that each succeeding word begins with the next letter of the alphabet. The translation, from the Rabbinical Assembly Mahzor, follows the same alphabetical pattern.

The leader asks members of the group to read through the Confessional. After a minute or two he then instructs members of the group to select three of the list of sins which the group member feels the strongest need to deny. In other words which of these three sins would you feel it most important for you to say, "I am not guilty of this." Which of these three would you feel most strongly that you did not commit during the past year. Underline those three.

The leader now asks each person to find a partner and to share those three. After a few minutes when everyone has shared with his partner the list of three sins he feels most compelled to deny, the leader continues. He may say something like this: "Among the things we have learned from depth psychology is that persons feel the strongest need to deny those things which are most often true. Think now of how you have indeed committed in some way the three sins which you felt most strongly the need to deny." The leader then asks each person to share, to the degree that he is comfortable, each person taking a turn. The leader may then ask members of the groups who wish to do so, to share some of the conversation with the whole group.

The leader may then ask members of the group to select three "sins" which are not found on the list, which they feel they are guilty of performing during the past year. After participants have had a chance to think about this and perhaps write it down, they are again asked to share these with the same partner.

This exercise may be followed by a self-contract which can be found in Activity Number 25 in the previous volume, Clarifying Jewish Values.

VIDUI-Confessional

Ashamnu bagadnu gazalnu dibarnu dofi.
He'evinu vehirshanu tafalnu shaker.
Ya'atznu ra, kizavnu latznu maradnu ni'atznu
sararnu'avinu pashanu tzararnu kishinu'oref.
Rashanu shihatnu ti'avnu ta'inu titanu.

We abuse, we betray, we are cruel.
We destroy, we embitter, we falsify.
We gossip, we hate, we insult.
We jeer, we kill, we lie.
We mock, we neglect, we oppress.
We pervert, we quarrel, we rebel.
We steal, we transgress, we are unkind.
We are violent, we are wicked, we are xenophobic.
We yield to evil, we are zealots for bad causes.

Reprinted from The Mahzor, ed. Jules Harlow. ©
The Rabbinical Assembly, 1972. Reprinted by permission

<u>An Experiential Exercise in Empathy</u>

This activity is designed to be used prior to or during the festival of Passover, but may be used effectively at any time during the year. It is a guided fantasy exercise and should be used with delicate care by a trained facilitator.

One of the major difficulties which educators have faced is the inability to convey to students the pathos and agony of oppression. Most often we talk about oppression but are not really able to feel the depth of pain, agony and anguish that accompanies it. Most teaching about Passover is "talking about" the holiday and very little <u>experiencing</u> the deeper meanings of the festival. It is clear that the ancient Rabbis understood the need for <u>experiencing</u> the meaning of the day. The entire Passover Seder is designed to be an experiential learning exercise during which the participants <u>feel</u> the meaning of the experience. Eating the matzos and the bitter herbs and the haroset, are all designed to help the celebrant to get into the mood of the festival, not just to understand it intellectually.

The leader asks the members of the group to find a comfortable position, to sit or lie down. He goes through some relaxation technique, asking the group to release any tension in their body and find themselves becoming completely relaxed. He then asks them to recall incidents in their childhood in which they felt humilitated, put down, disgraced, inhibited, or frustrated. What experiences come to your memory which are filled with unhappiness, pain, agony or frustration?

The leader allows five to seven minutes of quiet fantasy time during which participants conjure up such experiences.

Then the leader quietly tells the participants that whenever they are ready they may open their eyes and gradually return to this room and sit up. The leader then asks members of the group to list the feelings that they had during those experiences. The idea is not to recount in detail the experiences themselves, but merely to throw out one or two words or phrases which summarize the feeling level reactions which they had during those times. The leader then writes on the chalkboard or flip chart some twenty-five or thirty words (such as pain, anger, sorrow, frustration, inhibition, rage, terror, hurt, etc.) and the group is able to see this list very clearly. The leader may then ask the group to make a comparison between their own feelings and the feelings of the Israelites during the time of the Egyptian oppression, when they were building store houses, store cities and pyramids in Egyptian slavery.

This guided fantasy experience thus enables participants to truly feel the depth of despair of the oppressed Israelites during the period of Egyptian bondage through re-experiencing similar feelings of their own.

The leader is again reminded that guided fantasy exercises dealing with strong feelings must not be rushed but rather given the full amount of time to process and work through these strong feelings. A leader who is uncomfortable with the expression of the feelings on the part of the group should not lead such an exercise, because this lack of comfort will reflect itself and make it difficult for the group to handle its own feelings. However, with proper guidance this can be an extremely effective tool for the teaching of the deeper meanings and levels of Passover.

A Hannukah Exercise on Jewish Identity

This exercise consists of having participants complete eight sentences regarding their Jewish identity, one sentence for each branch of the Hannukah Menorah. It is best if the leader writes the beginning part of the sentence on the board or flip chart. The heading will be, "Because I am a Jew....". Underneath that will be the following phrases one under another.

I appreciate....
I demand....
I wonder....
I hope....
I need....
I should....
I will never....
I always....

Alternatively, the leader may prepare this sheet in advance on a ditto or mimeograph and hand out copies of "Because I am a Jew...." sheet and have participants fill in sentences right on that sheet. In either case allow approximately eight to ten minutes for participants to complete these sentences.

The next step is for each person to find a partner, perhaps someone he does not know well and would like to get to know better, and to exchange papers with the partner. Each person reads the eight sentences of his partner and is asked to look for a pattern in these eight sentences and then to say to the partner: "You seem to me to be the kind of person who....".

This will give the opportunity to participants to get a new perspective on their Jewish feelings and attitudes from a neutral, objective observer.

The final step in this exercise will be for each participant to write a few sentences describing himself in terms of his Jewishness, based on the eight sentences which he composed as well as the feedback he received from his partner. This can begin with the phrase: "I am the kind of Jew who....".

The leader may then call on several people to read their sentences.

Trust Exercises

The subject of trust in God and trust in the universe is one that is not dealt with effectively in most educational programs. It is a very difficult concept to talk about. The late Rabbi Heschel said that talking about God is like trying to bite into a wall. It is extraordinarily difficult to intellectualize about passionate commitments and feelings. The bias of this handbook is toward the experiential mode of learning which far more effectively reaches into the feeling level of the participants and enables the learning to come from within.

There are three trust exercises which can be used to help group members get in touch with their own sense of the ability to trust. First is the Trust Walk.

Each person finds a partner, taking turns leading the other person. Person A closes his eyes (or even more effectively has his eyes covered with a scarf) and is led around by the other person. This is best done in a large area such as outdoors. The leader should demonstrate how the person leads his unsighted partner by putting the right arm around the waist and the left arm holding the unsighted person's left arm. This procedure need not be followed throughout the experience but should be done in the beginning and at any point where there is a dangerous terrain. The unsighted person is led around approximately twenty to thirty minutes, although shorter periods may also be effective if circumstances do not permit a full half hour or if the surroundings are not large enough for that amount of time. At the end of the designated time the partners switch, the unsighted person becoming sighted and vice versa.

The group returns at a designated time and discusses how it felt to be without the capacity to see and whether or not they were able to trust their partners. Some further discussion might then be held to compare the participants' general ability to trust such as trust in God, trust in the Universe, trust in oneself, trust in friends and other people.

The next trust exercise is the Trust Fall. This exercise is also done with partners. One person stands behind the other and the person in front closes his eyes and falls backwards. The person behind catches the individual. It is best to try to catch the individual as close to the ground as possible, of course taking no chances that the individual may be physically harmed. This exercise should be done on a carpet or on the soft ground and not on a hard floor. A prior announcement should be made also that anyone with a bad back or other physical disability might decide to decline participation. Or they might watch others do it first before deciding whether or not they are physically able. Extreme caution should be taken so that no one is physically harmed.

The same processing as above can take place, having the person who fell describe his experience and compare this feeling with his general ability to trust.

The third trust experience consists of from eight to twelve persons standing around in a tightly knit circle with a focus person in the center, eyes closed, leaning against one individual. The focus person is then passed around the circle, forward and backward, with the members of the circle pushing that person to and fro taking care not to push too hard but merely have the person have the trust of the group's support. This exercise also should be done only by one who does not suffer physical disability.

These experiences can be very powerful learning strategies and sufficient time should be given for full processing by participants.

Surrogate Appreciations

This exercise is similar in some ways to Activity Number 56, Role Reversals. One of the general principles of Gestalt therapy is that every resentment also carries with it an appreciation. Every time a person resents an action or statement by another person there is also a hidden side of that resentment which is an appreciation of it. In most cases the appreciation is not expressed and most often not even realized. For the individual to be completely aware of his full range of his feelings, attitudes and values, it is important to be in touch, not only with one's resentments and demands, but also with the appreciation that accompanies them.

Each person finds a partner to work with and one person at a time will be given two minutes to express his appreciations. He must imagine during this exercise that he is speaking to someone with whom he has strong disagreements such as an Arab, a person of another faith or a person who disagrees with him on some important Jewish issue, or perhaps someone who belongs to a different group, movement or ideological school of thought. For example, he might validate an Arab. This means that for two minutes the person will speak to his partner as if he were an Arab expressing all the appreciations that are behind the resentments and demands that he makes under ordinary circumstances. That person might say something like, "I appreciate your courage to struggle for your homeland." "I appreciate your willingness to persist in the face of public criticism." "I appreciate your love of the land which you believe is yours." etc., etc..

One way to conduct such a surrogate appreciation exercise is to form groups of four within which two dyads begin to work with one another. For example, each person says to his partner some appreciations as if the other were an Arab. They each take a turn doing this for two minutes. At the end of this four minute sequences each person finds a new partner within his quartet and validates his partner as if he were a Christian. After that four minute sequence each person finds still a new partner within the same quartet and validates or appreciates his partner as if he were a member of another religious demonination such as Reform, Conservative, Reconstructionist or Orthodox. Alternatively, for the third partnership each individual may be allowed to select someone or some type of person with whom he disagrees strongly and expresses his appreciation.

Any other opposing role may be substituted for Arab, Christian, etc.

At the end of this exercise participants can be asked to share their learnings in terms of how it felt to say these things and what was going on inside them as they said them and immediately afterwards. Furthermore, what effect did these words seem to have on the listening person. Finally, what long range implications are there for these controversial issues and ideological disagreements among peoples and groups?

Adapted from another exercise I learned from Sidney B. Simon.

Jewish Assertiveness

This is an exercise frequently used in Assertiveness Training and has application for one's assertive style in connection with Jewish self-concept.

The leader says to the group: "We will now do an exercise that is somewhat risky. I need three volunteers to come out to the center of the circle (or to the front of the room)". The leader waits and if necessary gives some kind of encouragement so as to insure the fact that three people volunteer and come forward. The leader then scratches his head as if thinking further and then turns to the group and says, "I could actually use three more volunteers." He then waits for three more volunteers to come forward. He repeats the same procedure as if to be rethinking the situation, and turns to the group once more and says, "Alright, two more volunteers, this is the last group, just two more."

The leader then turns to the group and surprising them, says, "This is the end of the exercise!"

The leader explains that the point of the exercise was to determine and to help focus on one's assertive style. He then asks the members who volunteered: "What was going through your mind in deciding whether or not to volunteer?". After those people have responded he turns to those who did not volunteer and asks the same question to them.

The leader stresses the fact that we are not putting value judgments on whether or not one volunteered. We are merely giving ourselves an opportunity to see how easy it is for us to carry out our wishes. The question is not did we or did we not volunteer, but rather, were we able to do what we wanted to do. That is, if a person wanted to volunteer, was he able to do so and was he able to do so the first time or the second time or only after two groups had already volunteered. Conversely, if a person did not wish to volunteer, did he feel group pressure and did he indeed succumb to that pressure? To repeat, the question is whether one carries out one's wishes, whether one can be assertive in filling one's needs or not.

The leader then says to the group: "Having achieved a better view of our assertive style, let us now see if this has a relationship to our Jewish lives. What happens, for example, when someone tells an anti-Semic joke in our presence, not realizing that we are Jewish? What is our assertive style in that case? Or what happens when activities are schedules on Jewish holidays? Do we pretend, do we resist such scheduling, do we voice objections, or what exactly is our behavior? Are we able to carry out that which we intend and that which we desire?

The leader may then turn to the group to generate other similar instances and questions which test our assertive style in relationship to our Jewishness. After each question is raised or perhaps after a series of questions is generated, the leader may turn to members of the group and ask them how they would behave in similar circumstances.

Another possibility would be to have the group compose a questionnaire (instrument) testing one's Jewish Assertiveness Style.

The leader concludes the exercise by reminding participants that there is no right or wrong answer regarding volunteering or participating in community actions, but rather to be able to function without crippling embarrassment so that our needs are met. Being a member of a minority group strongly impinges upon our ability to function in a multi-cultural society.

Yes--No

This exercise like the previous one comes from the Assertiveness Training movement. Its purpose is to help participants get in closer touch with particular feelings regarding their anger, commitment to a cause, and/or depth of feeling regarding a particular issue. For our purposes the exercise can help group members become more fully aware of their inner feelings regarding some specific Jewish issues. The leader asks members of the group to form dyads. Each dyad decides who will be A and who will be B. A's start by saying yes and B's saying no That is the entire exercise. One says yes while the other partner says no.

Prior to this yes--no saying each person should get in touch with an affirmative or negative position on some Jewish question and have that in mind during the saying of yes or no.

For example: taking the most common realm of debate, the Middle East, the person saying yes might have in mind that he insists on retaining the occupied areas of the West Bank of the Jordan River. And so as he says yes he thinks of this particular issue. Another possibility is to think of one specific person while reciting the yes or no. One might picture the face of the Soviet Premier for example and think to himself while saying yes, "Yes, the Jews in Russia do deserve the right of emigration." A third possibility would be for a parent to be saying no to a child regarding the issues of interdating or intermarriage. The point is to have some issue or person in mind relating to one's Jewishness and then begin saying yes and the other person saying no. This is repeated for approximately three to five minutes holding the conversation merely with the words yes and no. Each person has his own issue in mind and does not reveal it to his partner.

At the end of the three to five minutes the partners may now switch, the yes now saying no and no now saying yes.

At this point the leader asks several members to explain in as much detail as possible their reactions, emotional and intellectual, to the exercise. Reactions will vary in content and intensity and may relate to the depth of feeling reached or to the increased self-awareness about the ability to assert oneself on specific Jewish issues.

"No Matter What You Say...."

   This is an exercise that comes out of the Human Potential Movement, particularly related to issues of self-concept. Here it is adapted to enhance one's Jewish self-image. It can be used in conjunction with Activity Number 37, the applauding and cheering at the sentence, "I am a Jew."

   The leader instructs the members of the group to recite in unison the following sentence, "No matter what you say or do to me I will always remain a proud Jew." The group then rehearses reciting this sentence in unison, "No matter what you say or do to me I will always remain a proud Jew." The leader asks the group to repeat this several times getting louder and louder, and tells them that after the first four or five times he will interject statements in between and they are to respond ever more strongly with the same sentence, "No matter what you say or do to me I will always remain a proud Jew."

   The group then recites this sentence four or five times, and the leader interjects the following statement and ones like it between the group's recitation:

   Jews are very pushy.
   All you care for is your own people.
   Money, wall to wall carpet and Cadillacs, that's all you Jews are good for
   Why don't you go move to Israel, you love it so much.
   Christ killers!

   The leader may utilize similar anti-Semitic phrases or ones that might have particular revelance to his own special group.

   The constant repetition of this sentence has the effect of planting a seed of pride and strength of self-defense within the participants. While many persons have felt this at first to be an artificial exercise with almost mechanical quality to it, after having performed it several times one begins to see the powerful effects that it has on those willing to try it.

Love Ball

This is an activity of physical contact which expresses a great deal of group affection and should be reserved for the proper level of readiness in the life of the group when participants feel close to one another. It might be utilized at the end of an evening or the close of a weekend or in any other appropriate way which the leader deems fit.

Members of the group are bunched together in the center of the room and form a very tightly knit unity, brushing up as closely as possible to the person in front as one can. At that point several persons begin to chant the word Shalom. The second syllable is often held for long periods of time. Other people at random begin to chant Shalom so that the word is constantly repeated and chanted again as a group refrain.

The emotional effect of this physical and verbal contact and unity can be extremely powerful and has the effect of drawing the members of the group even closer to one another, strengthening their shared ideals and feelings.

Full Length Mirror

This is a validation exercise. I use the word <u>validation</u> to mean <u>affirming</u> another human being, recognizing the worth in that person and in so doing, enhancing his very essence and helping him to feel better about himself. It is a common activity in self-concept enhancement workshops.

The group stands in a line or if the group is more than twelve or fifteen, then smaller groups of ten to fifteen are formed. This exercise works only if the persons know each other to some degree. It cannot be used in a group of strangers.

The first person in line goes down the line one by one spending one minute with each person acting as if he were a full length mirror reflecting some of the goodness and worthwhileness of that person. The individual who is moving down the line stands in front, face to face with the person, and states positive things about that individual. The focus here should include some of the person's positive Jewish qualities and Jewish commitments. For example the speaker might affirm the other person's involvement in the synagogue or in the Jewish community, or in Jewish study or Jewish worship, etc., etc.. After the first person has gone through the entire line taking one minute for validating each of the persons in the line, then he goes to his place and the second person repeats the entire process going through the entire line and so on until each person in the group has had a chance to do this.

The effect of validating and affirming other members of the group for their very essence as well as for their positive Jewish qualities has the effect of tightening Jewish consciousness as well as bringing members of the group much closer together and establishing warm, healthly relationships.

For other similar validation exercises see the writer's collection, <u>Teaching People To Love Themselves</u>.

Adapted from <u>Meditation For Children</u> by Debra Rozman (Millbrae, CA; Celestial Arts, 1976) page 140.

Back Rub Train

This is a very warm, touching exercise. It can be used when the group is tired and needs some relaxation and energizing. It can also be used at the end of an activity or the end of a program to reward the members of the group for their hard work in the previous time period.

Members of the group stand in a circle, then each person turns to the right so there is someone in front of him and someone in back of him. It is usually necessary to take one or two steps to the left to shrink the circle in order that everyone is able to reach the person in front of him. The next step is to place one's hands on the shoulder of the person in front and begin to give that person a shoulder message.

At this point there will be a lot of laughter expressing anxiety and uneasiness, which is perfectly normal. The leader may say at this point that it is best to let one's hands do all the talking and to remain silent. This helps create a more delicate and sensitive atmosphere for this caring exercise. The leader will probably have to repeat those directions two or three times to quiet down the members and finally a sense of quiet will reign and a nice serene, tender atmosphere will be created. The leader may say some sentences such as:

Help take all the tiredness out of the shoulders of the person in front of you. Wouldn't it be nice if the President began his cabinet meeting this way? People will probably laugh at that and become more relaxed and comfortable with the exercise.

The leader then asks the group without removing their hands to slowly come to a halt, keep their hands there on the shoulders of the person in front for a moment and very gently removing them so that the person hardly knows that they are gone.

The leader then says to the group: "Since you know how the person behind you likes to receive a message, let's all turn around and return the favor." Everyone will then do that, some more giggling will take place, and the leader will then remind the group to let their hands do all the talking. After three or four minutes the leader says again, "Without removing your hands let them come to a slow halt and then very gently remove them so that the person hardly knows that your hands are gone."

The leader may then say, "This is your reward for all the hard work we did today."

I learned this exercise from Sidney B. Simon. (See Simon's beautiful little book, Caring, Feeling, Touching, for similar exercises).

One Thing I Like About You

This is another validation exercise which is extremely helpful in creating a sense of group solidarity. It would be most effectively used in a group that has been together for some time, at least an hour or two so that people know something about the others in their group. It can be used in a small group of ten to fifteen.

Validation exercises in Jewish groups are very effective in helping members feel better about one another and feel more personally close to the other group members. This has the effect of tightening the ability to work on content issues and to grapple with Jewish problems with a sense of a covenant community. It does more than anything else possibly can to create the feeling of Klal Yisrael (Jewish unity).

Group members are sitting in a circle and the leader instructs one person to turn to the person at his right and say the following sentence, "One thing I like about you is...." and to complete that sentence. That person then turns to the person on his right and says the same thing and so on around the circle until the cycle has been completed. There is no need to process this further. The positive feelings that grow out of this exercise are so evident that they need very little further discussion.

It cannot be emphasized enough how important an atmosphere of warmth and mutual acceptance and mutual affirmation is in helping people feel the sense of Jewish community. It is in the last analysis this sense of community which helps persons feel the ultimate value of Jewish identity. The sense of belongingness, the sense of relatedness and connectedness are the first step in creating a meaningful Jewish community.

The High Priest Fantasy

This is a closure activity which helps point toward the future and creates a bridge from the program or workshop to the time following. It also helps to bridge the gap between knowledge and action, between midrash and maaseh, between study and deed.

As in all guided fantasies the participants are asked to get comfortable, relax and release any body tensions they may be aware of. The lights may also be dimmed.

The leader speaks as follows: See yourself located in the middle of a beautiful meadow. Look around and feel the warmth and the comfortable winds blowing on your face and see what kind of trees and bushes and plants are around you. Feel those feelings and get into that mood. (Pause). In the distance you see a large, tall mountain. Walk towards that mountain and go to the top of it. At the top you see a huge temple. Walk towards the temple and go inside. (Pause). Inside the temple on a high throne is sitting the Kohen Gadol, the High Priest. The High Priest is a wise, old, loving person. He beckons you to approach. Walk towards him, see the smile and caring on his face, see how comfortable it feels to be in his presence. (Pause). Now ask him the following question: "What is the next step in my Jewish growth and development?" See what answer the High Priest gives to you.

The leader then pauses for five to ten minutes so that participants can permit their fantasies to function and receive an answer from the High Priest.

The leader then continues: If the message from the High Priest is not clear, you may ask him questions to achieve greater clarity.

After two or three more minutes the leader then continues: Now it is time to go and the High Priest gives you a gift symbolizing the message that he spoke to you. Reach out your hand and accept this gift and look and see what it is.

The leader then pauses for another few moments to permit this part of the fantasy to take place.

The leader continues: Knowing that you can always return to the High Priest for any advice on any question that you have, you now turn and walk out of the temple, go down the mountain and return to the meadow. Feel your feet on the ground, feel the wind blowing in your face, feel the sun shining, bringing warmth and heppiness into your heart. Whenever you are ready open your eyes and slowly return to this room.

The facilitator pauses for another moment until everyone's eyes are open and ready to continue.

The leader may then call upon a number of people to relate their fantasies. And ask them to tell the message that they received as well as the gift which symbolizes it. In a small group of ten to fifteen it is good to hear from everyone. In a larger group the leader may want to form smaller groups of four to six so that everyone has a chance to tell about his fantasy.

Meditative Dyads

The purpose of this exercise is to summarize the learnings from a program, retreat or workshop. The group is broken into dyads. The leader tells the group that they will take turns sharing their learnings and their partner will record them in the person's notebook or on a separate piece of paper. Each dyad decides who is A and who is B and then follows these instructions:

A and B sit knee to knee, eye to eye, as close as is comfortable. If they wish they may make some physical contact by holding hands. Both A and B close their eyes and feel the energy moving back and forth between them. After a moment B takes up a pencil or pen and paper and A remains with eyes closed and B with eyes open, and B says to A: "What did you learn during this program (workshop, weekend, etc.)?" A replies, "I learned that. . . .". B continues to ask the same question again and again giving A the opportunity to think of all the things that he learned during the course of this workshop. This continues for approximately ten minutes. B records everything A says.

At this point the leader gives the group a one minute warning to wind up, then both members again close their eyes and if they wish make some physical contact, sit quietly and send their energy back and forth.

At this point A opens his eyes, takes up pen or pencil and paper and asks B, "What did you learn in this workshop?" B then begins to say sentences, "I learned that. . . .", "I learned that I. . . .", "I discovered. . . ." I relearned. . . .", "I was surprised that. . . .", etc. A continues to ask the same question giving B the opportunity to generate a long list of his learnings for approximately ten minutes. A records everything B says on B's paper.

At the end of this period the persons exchange their papers so that each person can take with him a summary of his learnings.

The leader may then ask several people to read some of their major learnings to the large group.

This is an exercise from Psychosynthesis, which I learned fr
Canfield.

Closing Circle

This is designed to be the final activity of a group at the end of the day, the end of a program or the end of a weekend. All the participants stand in a large circle. The leader may make some comments about the progress the members have made during the time they have been together and any other appropriate remarks he wishes to express. He may also want to read a poem or short line from some appropriate source which ties in with the theme of the program. One very popular reading which can be used is the anomymous poem, "All I Got Was Words".

Then the leader asks the group to express appreciations to each other in the following manner. Each person who desires will turn to the person whom he wants to express the appreciation, look at that person directly, and say his name and say the words, "I appreciate you, Bob, for....". Some appreciations may relate to things which individuals did for one another, or may relate to specific risks or areas of growth individuals have achieved during the course of the workshop, or any other small or large matter which might merit an appreciation. It is important for the leader to remind the group not to speak about the person but speak directly to the person, looking at him and stating his name. It is also good to remind the group that the best appreciations are those expressed to an individual, not the entire group. An appreciation given to everyone is in essence given to no one. The leader may then model giving of appreciations by saying one or two, and by doing so to get the ball rolling. It is important that other members of the group express their appreciations as they so wish without any specific order or instruction. The leader should allow ample time for this even permitting brief pauses while other people think of what they would like to say. It is important to take enough time so that everyone who wishes may have a chance to express one or more appreciations.

Then the group may sing one or more closing songs such as Hineh Ma Tov or Shalom Chaverim.

ALL I GOT WAS WORDS

Anomymous

When I was young and fancy free,
My folks had no fine clothes for me
All I got was words:

> Gott tzu danken
> Gott vet geben
> Zoln mir leben un zein gezunt

When I was wont to travel far,
They didn't provide for me a car
All I got was words:

> Geh gezunt
> Geh pamelech
> Hub a glickliche rayze

I wanted to increase my knowledge
But they couldn't send me to college
All I got was words:

> Hub saychel
> Zei nischt kein narr
> Torah iz di beste schorah

The years have flown - the world has turned,
Things I've gotten, things I've learned,
Yet I remember:

> Zog dem emes
> Gib tzedokah
> Hub rachmonas
> Zei a mensch!

All I got was words.

* * * * *

PART THREE   Design for
                    WORKSHOP ON THE JEWISH FAMILY

I - Coat-of-Arms

(See Activity #9, Clarifying Jewish Values)

1)   Something important about your primary family
2)   Something important about your present family
3)   Some Jewish ritual object that is meaningful to you
4)   A Jewish belief you would never change
5)   The name of a Jewish family that epitomizes for you
         what Jewishness means
6)   One word which summarizes the best qualities of Jewish
         families

II - Values Name Tag

(See Activity #26 in this book)

A Values Name Tag is a 5 x 8 card with the person's first name printed in large block letters in the center of the card. In each corner, the person writes: a) something great about me, b) why I am important in my family, c) something my family did together recently, d) a present I'd like to give my family.

III - Voting Questions

(See Activity #11, Clarifying Jewish Values)

1)   How many of you have 3 or more children?
2)   How many come from a Conservative synagogue? Orthodox?
         Reform? Reconstructionist?
3)   How many belong to a different kind of synagogue than the
         one you grew up in?
4)   How many have regrets about the way you raised your
         children?
5)   How many think parents should punish through spanking?
6)   How many wish you were more religiously observant?
7)   How many would like your child to be a Hebrew teacher?
         A Rabbi?
8)   How many ever thought of going on aliyah?
9)   How many would like to do more things with the family?
10)   How many think day schools are good for Jewish children?
11)   How many think Jews should have more children per family?
12)   How many know Jews who are active in ZPG (Zero
         Population Growth?
13)   How many think family members should share in decision
         making?
14)   How many think young couples are unprepared for marriage?

15) How many read a book on marriage in the last year?

16) How many think that living together before marriage is a good way to test a relationship?

17) How many think that the feminist movement has strengthened Jewish family life?

18) How many think your synagogue is a community of people who really care about each other?

19) How many think Jewish families are reluctant to go for help with problems?

20) How many think affluence has adversely affected Jewish family life?

21) How many think more Jewish education would help strengthen Jewish family life?

22) How many think Jewish teenagers have a stronger value system than their non-Jewish peers?

IV - Rank Orders

(See Activity #12, Clarifying Jewish Values)

Which is worse?
intermarriage; converting to Hare Krishna; being jailed for selling hard drugs

Which do you want most for your child (someone you know)?
financial prosperity; good health; a Ph. D.; personal happiness; an active Jewish life

Which contribures most to Jewish family life?
attending synagogue services together; Friday night meal together: open communication; mutual acceptance

Which has the most influence on the life of a child today?
Synagogue; home; school; friends, TV

Which do you remember most fondly?
a family trip; Pesach Seder; a family reunion; a wedding or bar mitzvah

(The above rank orders are prioritized & discussed in small groups. The facilitator can ask for "I learned...." statements).

V - Four Corners

(See Activity #33 in this book)

In each corner of the room is a sign on the wall: 1) traditional, 2) Zionist/secular/Hebraist, 3) liberal (Conservative-Reform), 4) Apathetic

Participants go to one of these stations, according to which kind of family they grew up in, and each person explains why he made that choice.

After a few minutes, groups of four are made, consisting of one person from each of the four stations. Each person shares what it was like in his home. (If there are two or three left over, they may sit in with another group of four).

One member of each group of four shares with the entire group some of the highlights of the group's discussion.

VI - Seed Sentences

(See Activity #4 in Clarifying Jewish Values)

Each person is given pen or pencil and paper, and completes the following sentence: A good Jewish family is....

Each person finds a partner, preferably someone he does not know well, or has not spoken to yet in this group, and shares his sentence. A few volunteers then read their sentence to the entire group.

The facilitator may write key words from these sentences on the chalkboard or flip chart.

VII - Inventory

(See Activity #1 in Clarifying Jewish Values)

Each person is given pen or pencil and paper, and lists ten ideal traits of an ideal Jewish family.

These ten traits are then coded as follows: Write M if my family has that trait; write D if you would like to develop that trait, or your family might like to; and in the third column write one thing you might do to strengthen that trait in your own family.

Groups of four are formed and each person shares his inventory and coding.

The facilitator then calls on a few people to make "I learned...." statements (see Clarifying Jewish Values, p. 20, pg. 5).

VIII - Proud Whip

(See Activity #6, Clarifying Jewish Values)

This activity can be done in small groups of 6 or 8, or in the larger group. Each person thinks (or writes) of something he did recently to contribute to the life of his family. He then says a sentence beginning "I'm proud that I....". Each person in the circle takes a turn.

Alternate topics for the Proud Whip: Something unique about my family; some of my family's strengths are...

IX - Brainstorming

(See Activity #53 in this book for the rules for brainstorming)

How many ways can we think of to strengthen Jewish family life today in North America?

X - Self-Contract

(See Activity #25 in Clarifying Jewish Values)

Several persons read their self-contracts to the group.

XI - Closing Circle

(See Activity #75 in this book)

JEWISH AND SINGLE

A Workshop Design by Rabbi David Spitz

A Saturday/Sunday workshop for unmarried, Jewish adults in their twenties and thirties to share their values, feelings, and experiences regarding dating and being single. The workshop focuses on personal growth, needs, feelings about self, relationship with other singles, and ideas about the Jewish community and about the Jewish way of life.

SCHEDULE

SHABBAT			SUNDAY		
coffee and ...	1:30-	1:45	coffee and.	9:00-	9:30
I. INTRODUCTION	1:45-	3:15	V. COMMUNICATION		
break	3:15-	3:30	SKILLS	9:30-	11:00
II. HUMAN RELATIONS			break	11:00-	11:15
SKILLS	3:30-	5:00	VI. IMPEDIMENTS TO		
break	5:00-	5:15	COMMUNICATION	11:15-	12:45
III. BETWEEN MEN			lunch	1:00-	2:00
AND WOMEN	5:15-	6:45	VII. NUDGERS, ET AL	2:00-	3:30
dinner, havdala	7:00-	8:30	break	3:30-	3:45
IV. MEETING INTER-			VIII. JEWISH		
ESTING PEOPLE	8:30-	10:00	IDENTIFICATION	3:45-	5:30

SESSION I: INTRODUCTION
GOALS

1. To generate a relaxed atmosphere.
2. To foster a trust relationship in which participants will feel comfortable.
3. To tell participants what will be expected of them and what will not.
4. To provide an overview of the workshop.

PROCEDURE

A. GREETINGS, GROUND RULES, AND GOALS: As participants come in they are given name cards and invited to have some refreshments. Facilitator invites participants to sit in circle, introduces him/herself, and introduces the workshop:

What image comes to mind when you hear the word "single"? For some, "single" may be associated with a swinging, care-free, happy-go-lucky life style (a bumper sticker I once saw read "Thank God I'm single"). For others, single may mean a lonely loser, longing to be snatched from solitude to the joys of marriage. During this workshop you will be exploring your feelings, needs, concerns, and self-image as single people.

Today in the United States, it is estimated that 30% of the adult population (50 million people) are single. Most are 20-34 years old. In that age group the percentage of Jewish singles is higher than that of non-Jews. What services might be provided? How can you help in securing these services?

As this workshop progresses, and you get to know about the participants, you will probably want to share things about yourself. You are not required to share anything that you do not wish to share. You have the option to "pass".

Also, there may be exercises in which you feel uneasy. Please bring any distress to the attention of the facilitator. I am available to be of help.

B. INTRODUCING SELVES: Find an object in your wallet, purse, or pocket (real or imaginary) that best typifies you. As a way of introducing yourself, show it to us and tell us what we might learn about you from it.

C. MORE INTRODUCTIONS: DYADIC SHARING: Find a partner. Tell your partner about one project you are presently engaged in. Then listen as your partner tells about a project he/she is engaged in. (After the dyads have had sufficient time, the facilitator invites those who wish, to tell the entire group about their project.) Facilitator asks participants to form another dyad. This time, share with your partners: "When I am alone, by myself, I most/least enjoy...." (Again facilitator samples responses.)

D. SOME VOTING QUESTIONS:
 -How many would have welcomed more time to listen to/talk with their partners?
 -How many feel they have already met someone they would enjoy exchanging conversation with later?
 -How many found that both times they were pickers/pickees?

SESSION II: HUMAN RELATIONS SKILLS
GOALS

1. To introduce the concept of "nourishing person".
2. To foster evaluation of participants' skills as nourishing persons.
3. To explore feelings connected with giving and receiving compliments.
4. To encourage realistic goals in what is wanted in a date.

PROCEDURE

A. NOURISHING PERSONS: Form groups of six. All of us have known persons that have helped us to grow. Close your eyes. Think of some "nourishing person" in your life. What specific qualities did he/she possess? Take turns now brainstorming these qualities in your group. Now with your group of six, form "cartwheels" (Three in center facing out, partners on the periphery forming the spokes of the cartwheel. Later, to move to the next partner those on the periphery will rotate to the next person counter clockwise.) Now, tell your partner the three characteristics you consider most important in a nourishing person. (When finished, facilitator samples responses.) Move to next partner. Tell your new partner of a time in your life when you received an encouraging remark. How did you feel about it? Was it helpful or not for your growth? (Again facilitator samples responses). Now rotate to your third (and final) partner. Tell your new partner of a time in your life when you received a put-down. How did you feel about it? Was it helpful or not for your growth? (Again after sufficient time has been allotted, the facilitator invites responses from the group. He/she suggests that the "put-down" is the vulture of human relations.)

B. THE COMPLIMENT: The Mishnah celebrates the fact that we are all different. "Man stamps many coins with the one seal and they are all like one another; but the king of Kings, the Holy One, blessed is he, has stamped every man with the seal of the first man, yet not one of them is like his fellow." (M. San. 4:5) Would that in our relationships with others we could show appreciation for this uniqueness! Most people have difficulty with compliments. Giving compliments is difficult, accepting compliments is even more difficult. Suppose we try it out. Would someone here be willing to give someone else a compliment? (Compliment is given.) What feelings did you (The complimentor) have giving the compliment? What feelings did you (the complimentee) have receiving the compliment? (Facilitator repeats exercise eliciting feelings about which compliments feel sincere, and reactions to compliments that show acceptance.)

C. I.A.L.A.C. (I Am Lovable and Capable) Tell the I.A.L.A.C. story (See: Simon, Sidney: "I Am Lovable and Capable: A modern allegory on the classical put-down", Argus Communications, 1974).

D. A BINTEL BRIEF: Jewish immigrants who came to the United States from Eastern Europe during the 1890-1900 immigration sometimes used the Yiddish press to find a mate. Today such "personals" can be found in such periodicals as the Village Voice and the Los Angeles Free Press. Here is an example:

TALL, non-charismatic, mobile, Chicago area bachelor, 35, seeks erratic, bizarre, slightly crazy female to re-ignite his zest for life and re-charge his battery.

Take a partner. Tell your partner what you might include in an advertisement advertising you.

SESSION III: BETWEEN MEN AND WOMEN
GOALS

1. To explore qualities desirable in a "significant other".
2. To learn what special qualities turn women on to men, and men on to women.

PROCEDURE

A. THE IDEAL DATE: Group is seated in circle. Facilitator asks participants to name one quality they deem important in a date. After the group has responded, the facilitator now asks for three qualities (from those named or not) that the participants deem the most important, and why. (Here there may be repetition.)

B. THE FISH BOWL: The men are asked to form a circle. The women are asked to sit outside the circle as unobstrusively as possible, as observers. The facilitator joins the circle of men and moderates a discussion on the qualities or actions of women that turn them on or turn them off. The women watch quietly, but are permitted to ask questions of the men after the discussion is over. Then the men and women change places and the roles are reversed.

C. DISCUSSION: The entire group again forms one large circle, and the facilitator invites discussion and observations about these two fish bowl exercises.

BETWEEN SESSIONS III AND IV

Dinner and havdala can be made particularly joyous by enlisting the participation of as many willing volunteers as possible. Those who are willing might help with the food, offer creative prayers in conjunction with the "motzi", lead the birkat ha-mazon, participate in havdala, or possibly put together a melave malke consisting of song leading and maybe even a mini-talent show.

SESSION IV: MEETING INTERESTING PEOPLE
GOALS

1. To explore new ways of meeting interesting people.
2. To improve communication skills.

PROCEDURE

A. EXPERIENCES WITH MEETING: The facilitator asks that groups of six be formed for the purpose of group interviews. Members of the groups take turns (about 2 minutes each) being interviewed regarding the way in which they met some interesting person in their lives. When they are done, the facilitator listens to some of the stories. He/she asks the group to form one large circle and some of these situations are role played. The facilitator asks about feelings at various stages of the role play. (To add some humor, additional role play volunteers may be used to portray the primary role players' "parent" or "child" ego states. This is also a good device to get at some of the more subtle feelings.

B. THE DATING GAME: A volunteer sits in the group circle, off from center facing out. Without his/her being able to see, three volunteers of the opposite sex are selected to sit in the center of the circle. With his/her back towards them so he/she cannot see who was selected, the first volunteer proceeds to interview the three for a date, referring to them as number one, number two, and number three. After he/she has made a selection, the facilitator questions why that particular choice was made and tries to get at feelings on the part of participants and audience. (This is a fun activity, and educational, and could if the group seems willing, be repeated several times.)

DAY II
SESSION V: COMMUNICATION SKILLS
GOALS

1. To foster accurate listening skills.
2. To explore the area of non-verbal communication.
3. To practice the skill of checking things out.

PROCEDURE

A. ICEBREAKER The facilitator asks if each participant will tell of one thing that happened in the group yesterday that was meaningful to them. (After everyone has had a chance to respond, the facilitator might comment on the type of activities in store for the group that day.)

B. ROGERIAN LISTENING: Good communication between men and women sometimes requires the ability to listen accurately to your partner and to "attend" to him/her. Jewish tradition describes such "attending" behavior: "If your wife is short, bend down and listen to her whisper." (b. B. M. 59a) "Beware of wronging your wife; she is easily hurt and her tears are ready." (ibid.) "Husbands must honor their wives more than themselves and treat them with tender consideration." (Maimonides: Shaaray Ha-Musar) "If you respect your husband like a king, he will treat you like a queen...." (Midrash).

For this exercise find a partner of the opposite sex (if possible). (Facilitator hands out situation cards so that in each dyad one partner has situations one and three and the other partner has situations two and four.) The facilitator then proceeds to read the first half of situation one.

It could go something like this: "It is a first date. Your new boy/girl friend has taken you to a party where there are many of his/her buddies...." Those with cards containing situation one read the remainder of the situation: "You are tired and bored with your date's friends. You are angry with your date for having brought you to the party and neglecting you. Yet you like your new friend and would not like to jeopardize the friendship. Your job is to communicate this to your friend (partner). (The facilitator explains that in Rogerian listening, the person listening must accurately describe the feelings expressed by the person who has just spoken, before he/she makes the next comment. If the communication is unclear, he/she may ask a "clarifying question".) Situation one is followed by observations concerning communication skills. Other situations are enacted as time permits.

C. NON-VERBAL COMMUNICATION: Women form a circle, men observe unobstrusively outside the circle (the fish bowl). Women discuss the non-verbal cues they receive from men that indicate whether they are interested or not in continuing the relationship.

When they are done, the men are given a chance to ask questions. Then the men

92

change places with the women and they discuss the non-verbal signals they receive from women concerning the relationship. After the women have had their opportunity to ask questions, the entire group forms one large circle and comment about this exercise.

SESSION VI: IMPEDIMENTS TO COMMUNICATION
GOALS

1. To examine different styles of human interaction.
2. To foster those qualities that make for a truly open and free relationship.

PROCEDURE

A. SOME STYLES OF INTERACTION: According to a Midrash, the interaction between couples is such a complicated matter, that God has been involved with this selection ever since creation:

> A matron once asked Rabbi Jose ben Halafta: "What has your God been doing since He finished making the world?" "He has been matching couples in marriage." was the reply.... The matron declared that she could so as much herself; nothing was easier than to couple any number of slaves with as many slave-girls.
> "You may think it easy," said Rabbi Jose, "but it is as difficult for God as dividing the Red Sea."
> The matron accordingly tried the experiment with a thousand males and as many females, setting them in rows and bidding this man take this woman, etc. The next morning they came to her, one with a broken head, another with gouged-out eyes, a third with a broken leg; one man saying "I don't want her." and a woman saying: "I don't want him." Thus was the matron constrained to say that the mating of man and woman was a task not unworthy of the intelligence of God. (Pesikta Buber, 11b-12a)

Here are some interaction sculptures suggested by Virginia Satir. As we discuss them, think about how they relate to people whom you know. (Sculptures are acted out and discussed).

Siamese: Sara and Bob were the last couple to go steady. They were so happy to have found each other that they vowed never to be separated. Wherever he goes, she goes....

50/50: Barb and Stan share everything 50/50 exactly. If Stan invites Barb to a party, Barb reciprocates by inviting Stan to a party. If Barb invites Stan to dinner, Stan feels he must invite Barb to dinner.

Master/Slave: Steven tells Sue how lucky she is to to out with him, every chance he has. Sue takes this abuse because she considers herself generally unattractive to men. She does everything Steven wants her to do.

Worship: Dick gets tongue-tied where it comes to Ilana. He has difficulty making his needs known, and generally feels uncomfortable in her presence.

(A variation might be a role play with these interaction styles.)

B. GROUP DISCUSSION: After the group has had a chance to think about the five
styles, the facilitator might lead a discussion on ways to avoid these patterns.
(He/she might lead into the T.A. concept of "games", "rackets", and "payoff"
and how they interfere with open communication.)

SESSION VII: THOSE WELL-MEANING NUDGERS
GOALS

1. To provide support to drooping egos.
2. To foster a more tolerant understanding of those nudgers singles love and
hate so well.

PROCEDURE

A. FROM OUT OF JEWISH TRADITION: That Jewish singles often sense an
undue pressure to get married has its roots in Jewish tradition. Fewer than fifty
verses from the beginning, the Torah quotes God as saying, "It is not good that
man should be alone; I shall make a mate for him." (Gen. 2:18) Six verses
later we are told: "Therefore shall a man leave his father and his mother, and
cleave unto his wife, and they shall be one flesh." The Bible speaks of the wives
of most of its personalities: Adam, Noah, Lot, Abraham, Isaac, Jacob, Moses,
etc. In fact the only biblical personality not married is Jeremiah (see Jer. 16:2).
Of the many rabbis of the Talmud, only one, Rabbi Simeon ben Azzai, a disciple
of the renouned Rabbi Akiba, is reported as being a bachelor, and apparently at
times found himself on the defense. He explained: "But what shall I do, seeing
that my soul is in love with the Torah; the world can be carried on by others."

B. THE SHEILA LEVINE SAGA: In the comic novel "Sheila Levine is Dead and
Living in New York", Gail Parent portrays the norm of being married as it
effects one woman: Sheila Levine.

Sheila Writes: It's not only the parents' fault. I heard it everywhere. I read
Dick and Jane, and they had a mommy and a daddy who were married. Noah's
ark, they came two by two. Everything comes in pairs but Sheila Levine.
"What do you want to be when you grow up, Sheila?".... "I want to be a wife
and a mommy...." "Good Girl."

Yes, I learned at a very early age that I had better get married. A Jewish
mother wants her sons out of the army and her daughters down the aisle.

For this exercise we will need three people to be Sheila (Sheila could also be played
by a man, in which case we can call him Shelly Levine.) We will need three people
to be Sheila's mother or father. Each of the pairs (Sheila and parent) is given
a situation card and allowed a few minutes to prepare their script. Here are the
three possible situations. They are not taken from the Sheila Levine.... book
but rather are invented from areas the facilitator would like to open to
discussion. (With each role play, the facilitator tries to have some discussion
about feelings evoked. To dramatize the role of self-image, additional players
may be used to portray Sheila's self-image, and Sheila's parent's self-image.)

1. Saturday night is approaching and Sheila has not been invited out on a date.
2. Sheila returns home from a date with a boy her parents would like to see her
marry. Sheila has had a miserable time and does not want to see him again.
Her parents, however, are convinced that it is all her fault.
3. Sheila falls in love with a non-Jew and wants to marry him. Her parents
object.

SESSION VIII: JEWISH IDENTIFICATION
GOALS

1. To develop ideas of how singles can maintain their identification as Jews.
2. To stimulate more participation by singles in Jewish communal activities.
3. To encourage a wider selection of activities sensitive to the needs of Jewish singles.

PROCEDURE

A. BRAINSTORMING: Find a partner. Tell your dyad about the most memorable Sabbath or Festival you experienced as an adult. When dyads are ready, the facilitator listens to some of the experiences shared. He/she then asks that each dyad joins with another dyad forming a foursome. Switch partners. Tell your new partner how being single effects your observance as a Jew. When dyads are ready, the facilitator listens to some of the ideas. He/she then asks them to regroup as a foursome, and brainstorm about special ways singles can maintain their identification as Jews. The facilitator listens to some of the ideas, and then asks if the groups would brainstorm about services and community activities that would be useful and enjoyable to Jewish singles. Who would be best able to offer them? Again the facilitator listens to some of the ideas.

B. CONCLUSION: Facilitator asks participants to form a circle. Participants take turns completing the sentence, "From this workshop I have gained...."

FRIENDSHIP CIRCLE

SHALOM

EXPERIENTIAL LEARNING

Dr. Dov Peretz Elkins is a pioneer in the field of religious education and human development. He combines the wisdom, experience, training and insight of the talmudic sage and the modern behavioral scientist.

He has produced a series of important and valuable volumes on a new, exciting, challenging, and growth-producing way to learn. To learn about religion, the Jewish People, about yourself, about how to establish meaningful relationships, how to strengthen Jewish family life, and about the art/science of mench-ology (how to become a "mench" - a self-actualizing, fully-mature fully functioning human being).

Dr. Elkins

Finally,
A
New, Exciting
And Enjoyable
Way To Learn

Send order form below to: Growth Associates, Human Relations Consultants and Publishers, Box 8429, Rochester, NY 14618, 716/244-1225.

Quantity	Titles by Dr. Elkins	Price
	Twenty Experiential Programs for Jewish Groups $10.	
	Clarifying Jewish Values: Values Activities for Jewish Groups $10.	
	Jewish Consciousness Raising: 50 Experiential Exercises $10.	
	Loving My Jewishness: Jewish Self-Pride & Self-Esteem $10.	
	Humanizing Jewish Life: Judaism & the Human Potential Movement $12.	
	Teaching People to Love Themselves: A Leader's Handbook of Theory & Technique for Self-Esteem Training $17.50	
	Glad To Be Me: Building Self-Esteem in Yourself & Others $6.50	

	Casette Tapes ($7.50 each)
	  C-1 Creative Jewish Programming
	  C-2 Havurot: Program Development
	  C-3 Experiential Learning: Practice & Theory
	  C-4 Be Glad to Be You - The Magic of Self-Esteem
	  C-5 The Jewish Family: The Need for New Educational Programs
	  C-6 The New Judaism: Hasidism, Reconstructionism and Humanistic Psychology	

	The Ideal Jew: A Value Clarification Program (Leader's Guide & 15 participants' forms) $4.95.	
	"New Age Judaism" - Packet of articles & lectures on the theory and practice of Experiential Learning (written since **Humanizing Jewish Life**) $3.00.	

Name ....   Subtotal _____

Address ....   NY residents add 7% tax _____

City .... State .... Zip ......   TOTAL ORDER _____

All orders **must** be prepaid. Prices include postage & handling.   (Canadians please use US funds)

☐ Check **here** if interested in information on lectures, workshops and/or other training events.